A PRIVATE VIEWING

Barely out of his teens, W. R. Garrett found himself in North Africa on his way to join the Eighth Army. The former country boy, with idealistic views of why he was fighting, couldn't possibly have known the implications. He was to learn – quickly. He and his comrades didn't understand, until it was all over, that their brutal encounters with Germans and Italians had contributed to the rout of Rommel at El Alamein. This is the story of one man's war, and his later service, as a member of the Military Police, throughout the Middle East.

A PRIVATE VIEWING

A PRIVATE VIEWING

by

W. R. Garrett

Dales Large Print Books
Long Preston, North Yorkshire,
BD23 4ND, England.

British Library Cataloguing in Publication Data.

Garrett, W. R.
  A private viewing.

KENT
ARTS & LIBRARIES

A catalogue record of this book is
available from the British Library

ISBN   1-84262-433-4 pbk
ISBN   978-1-84262-433-3 pbk

First published in Great Britain 2004 by The Book Guild Ltd.

Published in Large Print 2006 by arrangement with
The Book Guild Ltd.

Dales Large Print is an imprint of Library Magna Books Ltd.

Printed and bound in Great Britain by
T.J. (International) Ltd., Cornwall, PL28 8RW

Off to War

It was really happening at last, though I viewed it with suspended belief. A long column of military vehicles trundled westward along the Egyptian coastal road. It was mid-August in 1942 and the 133rd Infantry Brigade was on its way to join the Eighth Army in a 'forward area'.

In the rear of an Army truck there was little to do but think or sleep and the more thought I applied to the situation the more unreal it seemed to be and my heart sank as the realisation grew that over two years of Army training had failed to prepare me inwardly for the imminent realities of war.

19 years of age on the outbreak of hostilities, I had contemplated meeting the war with a natural innocent excitement. The prospect, in so sound a cause, promised travel, comradeship and adventure and young men have a duty and there was no sin in welcoming that duty or in the desire to be tested in battle, however it may come.

Conscripted at the age of 20 years to Devizes barracks in Wiltshire, the shock of initiation into the vicissitudes of Army life was soon overcome. Still undergoing recruit training, I witnessed the reception of men from the beaches of Dunkirk who arrived, exhausted, late at night. It was a distressing experience, accustomed as we were becoming to a meticulous turnout, precision drilling and everything in kit-inspection order, to see this dishevelled ragbag motley of an army in total disarray. Royal Artillery men, Signal Corps men, sailors, infantry from diverse regiments and Air Force personnel all jostled for a place to rest and an opportunity to remove their weird assortment of dirty sea-water-stained clothing and to sleep in safety. Their condition spoke volumes about the evacuation and the military disaster that preceded it.

As we bounced and rattled along that notorious Egyptian road, the condition of which made sleep difficult to achieve, and had inspired the current joke about the builder of it being still in prison, I recalled the previous two years of Army service in the manner of a condemned prisoner reviewing his misspent life.

Three weeks previously we were still at sea, nearing the completion of a two month voyage from Liverpool. Most of our training had been endured in Yorkshire, tramping around moors and villages and sleeping rough under hedgerows, often in the rain. After recruit training, and mass inter-regimental transfers of personnel, I had become a member of the Royal Sussex Regiment and the rigours of Yorkshire saw the birth of the spirit and comradeship that moulds a battalion of strangers into a composite and durable entity.

From thence to Sussex and Kent and the potential invasion beaches and night man-oeuvres among the farms and orchards. Being country born and reared, and com-mendably fit and strong, I enjoyed the Spartan life. There were no physical prob-lems for me but deep within me lurked persistent anxiety. How would I react to war when I faced it in reality?

An infantryman's best friend we were told was his rifle. I grew proficient in its use, could route march, drill and sentry-go with the best of the rest, and was proud to be a private in the Royal Sussex Regiment, but the inner misgivings remained.

Travelling around the verdant shires of England thrilled me and the prospect of eventually setting foot in foreign lands was an exciting fantasy now made possible. The fortunes of war went from bad to worse overseas and a change of scene became more and more a certainty for all of us. When we arrived on the quayside at Liverpool and gazed in awe at the United States ship *Santa Rosa*, huge and beautiful and waiting, I knew fantasy was becoming greater than reality.

The voyage was an unforgettable adventure. The huge convoy assembled off the coast of Northern Ireland and ploughed its lonely way across the vast rolling seas like a tribe of marine nomads migrating to new feeding grounds. The gales blew, the ocean heaved, the *Santa Rosa* dipped, rolled and shuddered and over 2,000 soldiers were sick while the American crew hosed the decks and passed disparaging remarks about our manners.

How inviting the land appeared from the ship's deck! The sheer beauty of Freetown was breathtaking after two slow weeks at sea and after six days in the harbour, a vivid memory for the next two weeks voyaging to Cape Town. Ashore here, we learned to march again and our nostrils were treated to the forgotten scents of fresh citrus fruit. A beautiful and welcoming place we were reluctant to leave. Sailing to the north there was no secret now about our destination. Tobruk had fallen, the Eighth Army was back as far as El Alamein and only 70 miles of nothing much separated the Afrika Korps from Cairo, Alexandria, the Suez Canal and the vast empty regions of the whole Middle East and its precious oilfields. We sailed quietly through the Red Sea in late July duly thankful the U-Boats had failed in their nefarious task so completely.

The desert can be a cruel environment,

yet seasoned soldiers developed a strange love of 'the blue' as they termed it. Just how cruel it could be we were soon to discover, Learning to love it needed more time. There were few obvious physical attractions, though the sunrises and sunsets were glorious to observe, as they spread their mantles of splendour over the mysterious void.

The daytime heat and nightly chill, the yellow glare of endless sand unrelieved by a sight of greenery, the swarms of flies and the absence of water or sustenance of any kind combined to create a hostile world. It was punishing to skin and stomach and to young and inexperienced men from England's green and pleasant land it was frightening to contemplate.

As we left the coastal road to follow a mere track the menacing void rose up in great choking clouds of dust and engulfed us and blotted out all vision of the way back. Mile after mile of lonely empty desert reeled away behind us. Limitless, silent and mysterious, it was swallowing us relentlessly and our previous existence had lost any relevance. In the front of the column was someone who knew where to go and, with the aid of a compass, how to get there. The rest of us travelled hopefully in the certain knowledge that, uncomfortable as it was, it would be better than arriving.

An overnight stop before reaching our

destination provided an opportunity to view our environment and attune our mental attitudes. The infinite vastness and emptiness fostered a dangerous illusion of freedom and offered an open invitation to go anywhere in any direction without let or hindrance. Yield to the temptation and one could be lost for ever. There was a spiritual attraction. All-embracing, abstract, silent and unchanged for aeons of time, there was an atmosphere of sanctity. Void of earthly circumstances, it was a sanctuary of the spirit and the only inhabitant was God himself. With our obscenities of war we desecrated the holy peacefulness but in the immensity of time surely our intrusion bore the significance of a grain of sand. 'Time like an ever rolling stream, bears all its sons away.'

'Beware of the Hun'

We reached our destination early the next day. It would be inappropriate to suggest we arrived. Arrival suggests a completed achievement, an occasion. There was nothing to signify arrival. We stopped and the journey was over.

Gradually our situation assumed a shape

and meaning. We were on the southern end of a rocky ridge about 300 feet above the surrounding desert. To the south and west lay a vast yawning wilderness and forming a far distant horizon another lonely ridge could be discerned. These ridges bore names on the Army maps that soon became familiar to us and to the world. We were on the Alam Halfa ridge. Beyond was Himeimat ridge. I soon acquired a fascination for Himeimat, akin to a rabbit's fascination for a stoat for thereon we learned sat the dreaded Afrika Korps, looking across the shimmering miles in our direction.

The Eighth Army was under new management. The new commander was a General Montgomery. He was unknown to the desert veterans but we had served under him in South-East England and a more dedicated leader could not have been chosen. He insisted on all ranks being 'put in the picture' as much as possible and the gist of the message on Alam Halfa was – dig.

It was confidently expected that the enemy would attack in the region when the moon was full in ten days' time. Ten days to fortify the ridge sounded enough but these were desert conditions at their worst. We were a small detachment detailed for the defence of the Brigade Headquarters which required slit trenches, weapon pits, vehicle and gun positions, all of which had to be hewn out of rock.

Our rations were bad, corned beef and biscuits and little else served with a sprinkling of sand and garnished with flies. Half a gallon of brackish water for all purposes per man per day. This inevitably led to stomach disorders, a raging thirst and filthy clothes. Above all in terms of torment were the flies. Flies swarmed around us the whole day, seeking moisture in our eyes, mouths and ears. The work was demoralising. Picks and shovels were our only tools and were soon blunted on the unyielding rock. We welcomed the nights and a respite from the torment and toil and sweat. We welcomed the sunrise for its relief from the night's chill. Cuts and abrasions, and there were many, were constantly covered in flies and sand and developed into 'desert sores' that festered and refused to heal. If bandaged the flies would penetrate between the folds and search for blood.

The worse conditions become, the more the British soldier laughs but there were few who could raise a chuckle on Alam Halfa ridge.

There was one who could. One whose friendship I treasured. John Peters was a slightly-built young man who married shortly before our embarkation. As we swung our pickaxes and wielded our shovels and swiped at the accursed flies, he would be chattering

14

in chirpy fashion about his bride, Winifred, his home in Redhill, his job in the printing trade and though basically he was as miserable as the rest of us he would somehow manage to laugh. His comradeship was beyond price and with his help I retained my sanity. We worked together, grumbled together and with any luck would return to our homeland together. The soul-destroying conditions revealed how great and enduring can be the spirits of men. It was comradeship and tolerance and discipline that sustained us. There were good old English names in that foreign place. Tom Hughes, Danny Alford, Billie Potter, Alfred Cannings – wonderful people all and many others now the victims of a faulty memory.

Ten days of this standard of existence without respite was a daunting prospect. We had the appearance of a sick and sorry outfit. Secretly I longed for the battle to start, anything in fact to end the dreary routine. Fear would sometimes rise in our hearts as we contemplated our pathetic efforts at fortifying Brigade Headquarters. Slit trenches were too shallow, weapon pits inadequate and the situation that would present itself if the 21st Panzer Division loomed over the crest of the ridge on its way to Cairo defied description.

In an effort to complete the task in time, Royal Engineers tried to help with explosives.

This had the effect of destroying what little shape or form we had wrested from the rock and adding little to the depth. It all seemed quite hopeless and we despairingly slogged on in our own primitive and painful way.

The full moon was due on the night of August 27th. That day our defences looked terrible and so did we. There had been cases of dysentery and lesser ailments were thinning our ranks. Desert sores could no longer be bandaged because the Medical Officer needed to preserve his stocks for the anticipated action. Our khaki drill was filthy through lack of water. Wash a shirt in petrol and it soon disintegrates but it does kill the lice.

The full moon bathed the appointed battle venue in its pale ghostly radiance. Unfortunately no one came to share its romantic glow. General Rommel was cursed loud and long for failing to keep the appointment as we struggled through another day of fly-tormented toil and by August 30th we were even more dispirited by the thought of our ordeal having been entirely in vain.

At 2.00 a.m. on August 31st we were ordered to 'stand-to' and there we duly stood in the chilly gloom until the dawn and a spectacular sunrise heralded yet another day and after even less sleep than was usual the promise of another stint of arduous toil. August 31st however was to be a different

16

sort of day. Having been detailed to guard a stock of Quartermaster's Stores that had temporarily been dumped about 100 yards from our worksite, John Peters and I were parted for the day and my gratitude for thus escaping the daily grind knew no bounds. My eyes were drawn hypnotically across the empty wilderness to distant Himeimat Ridge as I ambled restfully among the assorted stores while my friends continued to hack away at their hopeless task.

There had been in recent days some sporadic air activity over Alam Halfa. High-level encounters between fighter planes and what had become known as the 'shuttle service'. Formations of British and American bomber planes with a fighter escort would pass overhead on a calculated course and at a calculated moment would unload their lethal cargoes, to be followed by another relay. The 'shuttle service' was providing a more frequent delivery sequence as I gazed across the intervening miles and being now nearer the crest of the ridge the actual delivery could be witnessed. A section of the horizon would erupt into a soaring dust cloud and in seconds a low rumbling sound of multiple explosions could be heard and the bomber formation would be seen as distant dots growing larger as they returned. Back and forth they flew like aerial refuse vehicles dumping their rubbish on the local tip.

Though it was in the interest of us all that those at the receiving end of the shuttle service system should be blown to pieces, I felt a twinge of compassion for them. It appeared and sounded a ruthless bombardment even at the considerable distance involved but nevertheless the fewer people who came to view our awful defence works the better it would be. It was an opportunity to test my aircraft recognition skills and an unfamiliar engine sound at almost 11.30 a.m. promised to be of similar interest. Shading my eyes the better to see the planes, the glare of the sun prevented any sighting.

'Beware the Hun in the sun' we had often been warned. Perhaps our privations had dulled my wits. Perhaps I had forgotten the unexplained emergency 'stand-to'. Perhaps I was still suspending belief in real events but there was no doubt in my mind I could differentiate between a Hurricane and a Kittyhawk if only they could be seen. An engine roar of increased pitch and intensity then emanated from the dazzling heavens. It heightened to a snarling scream and at last my aircraft recognition knowledge worked for me. I had heard that sound on newsreel and film. 'Stukas'! Not just one but a Stuka 'party'.

In a moment of desperate indecision I spun round to see how my friends with their

18

picks and shovels were reacting. They were all vanishing like rabbits going to ground and even as I started running I knew it was too late. The slit trenches, albeit too shallow, were too far away. Being in no mental state to make considered decisions some inner 'automatic pilot' threw me prostrate on the sand and the war erupted all around me with searing, shattering violence.

Detonating fragmentation bombs, cannon shells, ricocheting bullets and the whine of flying metal, screaming aircraft engines and anti-aircraft guns combined in a demonic symphony of destruction. With teeth clenched and muscles screwed into knots in anticipation of the mortal blow that could come any second, all earthly consciousness left my mind. I abandoned my earthly existence as though it had never been.

I prayed a simple prayer, 'Oh God!, Oh God!, Oh God!' over and over again.

Not a prayer for earthly deliverance but for spiritual acceptance and a spiritual hand to hold.

A glow of warmth spread through my body. Miraculously my fears had left me. I was safe. Nothing would hit me. All I needed to do was to stay flat and await the end of the onslaught. Time and physical realities were suspended and my mind was in limbo until the war crowded back into my being, deafening me. I had seen nothing of it and, seized by an irresistible urge to witness events, I raised my face from the sand and turned my head and stole a glance skywards. A huge towering pall of dust and black smoke from burning vehicles almost blotted out the sun that appeared as a pale disc as through an English November fog. The next Stuka in the queue was on its screaming passage and I heard the bomb coming. There was a vicious red flash and an ear-splitting crack as it exploded so near I could smell it. As I slammed my face back into the gritty sand a shower of metal fragments whined and fluttered over me. It should surely have blown my head off. I waited for the end of the onslaught which was followed by an utter silence such as only a desert knows. All creation was holding its breath.

The Loser

My mind in turmoil, slowly rising to my feet, I turned and sat trembling on a box of am-munition, which, like the cans of petrol, was part of the stores in my charge. Their lethal propensities had escaped my attention. The wonder of the experience at that moment was incomprehensible, my thoughts too disordered, too jumbled to form a sequential pattern. What of my friends? Turning to the direction of Brigade Headquarters, there was nothing to see but a slowly drifting cloud of black smoke and dust. So I was spared the sight of John Peters lying mortally wounded amid the hellish noise and confusion, spared the task of lifting him into the back of a jeep and holding him as it bounced across the pitted surface towards the casualty station. I should have been with him, and would have been with him, but was spared it all.

Later on that fateful day the Stukas returned. Their banshee howls came out of the sun as before. A less severe attack than the first, we all reacted faster and there were no casualties among our numbers. Nightfall brought safety and an opportunity to meditate on the lessons of the day. Since my recruit days I had tried to imagine meeting the war. As events propelled me nearer to it the conviction lingered on that it would never happen. On August 31st it did happen. We were all young soldiers experiencing enemy for the first time and we matured to some degree that day.

We waited in the darkness for news of our friend John. Mention of his name was painful and would initiate a struggle to hide the tears. News when it reached us was brutal in its finality. He had been buried before sundown we knew not where. A great sorrow filled our hearts and the tears flowed freely.

21

So ended our first day of war. A beginning and nothing more, but its effect upon us was permanent. No more disbelief, no more fantasising for me. There was a feeling of new-born confidence abroad and the bitterness of the day hardened us all. There was no purpose grieving too long for John Peters. There would be no more hardship or fear for John. In any case, he was an indestructible spirit. He was still living. Laughing too.

The Luftwaffe had 'put us in the picture'. The Panzer divisions were on their way. We manned our defective defence positions with some misgivings and waited. Set well back from the crest of the ridge, we were unable to see the valley floor. Battle was joined so near but out of sight. The German armoured forces had three options: to pass the ridge on the left or the right side or drive straight at it. The first two options were barred by British tanks in 'hull-down' positions and under orders not to be enticed into the open to be slaughtered. For two days the din of raging battle filled the desert air and we could only listen and hope. Then in desperation the frustrated General Rommel turned his tanks towards the ridge.

Our trepidations increased by the hour as stray armour piercing shells and bullets whined over our heads. We received frequent attentions from Stuka 'parties' but we used their diving screams as fire alarms and, duly warned, went promptly to ground. Montgomery had completely outwitted the old Desert Fox whose tanks were soon snarled up in minefields and artillery, anti-tank guns and aircraft sprang the trap and dealt a terrible retribution.

The shuttle service swarmed over in frequent relays. Owing to the dangerous proximity of their target to our position, an aircraft recognition sign had been devised for our protection. A collection of petrol cans cut into halves and filled with sand were laid out to form a large letter W. Soaked in petrol and ignited, the mixture would burn for a considerable time and guide the shuttle bombers from us. With the battle raging so near the foot of the ridge, it was eventually deemed expedient to light it. Armed with a box of matches, a companion and myself set out to traverse the open ridge to apply the flame to our primitive innovation. The next formation of bombers thundered overhead and to my heart-stopping horror there came the whistle of falling bombs. There was time only to fall flat as a string of heavy bombs fell across Brigade Headquarters with a blast and concussion that was frightful. Fortunately only one plane made the error. The others delivered their bombs to the correct address while we raced back to our trenches. The whole idea of the flaming signal was abandoned and it could possibly be there now still waiting for a match.

Two of our men were hit by flying metal and left for the comforts of hospital and we forgave the Royal Air Force for the error of their ways. Instead we blamed the hateful fly-blown hell of a place it was our misfortune to be billeted in.

The enemy losses were severe, their fuel was running out and their luck had already done so, and they opted for their final choice – they fled whence they came. The British tanks refused to be drawn into the open and both forces lived to fight again another day. Soon perhaps.

A few days later we departed in a North-Easterly direction. As Alam Halfa ridge receded into our memories, thoughts crowded into my mind. Our war initiation rites were over. The shock and tragedy was being absorbed as a boxer absorbs a body blow. As the dust rose from our wheels and hid the dreadful ridge from our eyes, my thoughts were of Surrey with its lush green swards and Jersey cows, its hedgerows, trees and flowers and bird song. The corn harvest would be in full swing in that fair land where life is governed by the four seasons and in lovely Redhill dwelt the tragic and sorrowing Winifred, not long a bride, so soon a widow. It could be argued that the battle of Alam Halfa had no real winner. So be it. It had a loser.

A Scottish Overture

Our return journey ended in sight of the Mediterranean Sea. It was gloriously blue and its invitation was undeniable. We threw ourselves into it at the first opportunity and wallowed in the chilly freshness of its embrace, emerging clean and rejuvenated. Most of our days were spent cleaning our equipment, our clothes and ourselves, resting, sleeping and living a little. There were very few flies to torment us and various theories were advanced to explain the enormous fly population on Alam Halfa ridge, all of which were equally revolting.

Our holiday lasted six days and then we were back into the depths of the desert and training was the order of the day and often the night. We were now acquiring that love of 'the blue' so peculiar to British soldiers. The miseries and suffering of Alam Halfa were behind us and our circumstances were less harsh. Also we were constantly on the move and travelling across the endless wilderness was a great attraction, like journeying through time and space. Its distant horizons were ever inviting and to stop in one spot for long invited only tedium. There perhaps lay the secret – to be nomadic. All desert dwellers are nomads. Certainly no self-respecting Bedouin Arabs would have set camp on Alam Halfa.

General Montgomery was an ardent trainer of soldiers. We had memories of his famous all-ranks cross-country runs in Kent where he had us all galloping around in ever-increasing circles. His new command had not changed his views and he was thinking ahead to a future battle, as indeed we all were. The timing was now common knowledge. The next full moon, October 23rd. As the day approached the excitement mounted in the Eighth Army. The new Commander had instilled a great new spirit. His messages – 'to be read to all ranks' – laid his own reputation on the line. The vital necessity of victory and the absolute catastrophe of anything less was obvious to all.

The 40-mile bottleneck between the sea at El Alamein and the impenetrable Quattara Depression, ordained by Fate countless ages ago, was the only region where an exhausted and dispirited Desert Army had been able to hold the victorious Afrika Korps. It was a gift from Creation.

The Allies stood with their backs to a great oil supply and the port of Suez. The

Germans were thousands of miles from their supply sources. The elements of victory were there but the coming battle would be the last chance. The situation was unique in history and all were conscious that we were to play a part in an event of immense historical importance.

Fate had also fashioned General Montgomery's career to make him precisely the type of leader for the occasion and a mood of eager optimism prevailed. The enemy flood had been checked at Alam Halfa. The tide would be turned at El Alamein. Montgomery had said so.

In the late evening of October 21st we lay wrapped in our blankets waiting for sleep. It was a quiet tranquil evening and the warmth of the day still lingered when we heard a magical sound in the clear desert air. The skirl of bagpipes. The piper was inspired and the familiar and much loved notes from a medley of Scottish airs drifted across the desert on a wave of enchantment. It raised a surge of emotion in all who heard it.

The Highlanders were across there somewhere – the Jocks! It was a splendid and moving Overture to the Battle of El Alamein and we slept soundly that night.

The following day we moved towards the battle line – to our starting point – and made our final preparations. Preparations for we knew not what. We had certainly grown up since our uncomfortable journey to Alam Halfa. The change in attitudes was striking. There was excitement where unspoken fear prevailed before. In Eighth Army parlance, we had 'got our knees brown'. Our previous experience was as nothing to the ordeal others had endured but come what may we were ready, whereas before we never were. Our rather cocky confidence may have appeared foolhardy to our elders. It was not easy to explain, it was wholly illogical. We resented some of the desert veterans who predicted 'just another complete cockup', but we were relatively raw and had not endured the demoralising experience of disaster and retreat. There was, however, something in the air. A Faith. We could not fail, it was unthinkable. No one imagined it would be easy. There was great respect for the enemy whose fighting qualities were only too well known. Rommel was not known as the Desert Fox for nothing but the Alamein line was not ground of his choosing. It could not be outflanked in any way and resembled to a degree the First World War with two opposing Armies dug in and facing each other with a frontal assault the only way to move. It would not be a battle of manoeuvre and movement but a stand-up slogging match with infantry and artillery playing major roles. Montgomery was an infantryman from the First World War days. Rommel was a tank warfare expert who favoured mobility and space.

So it came to pass that we waited almost with bated breath for 9.40 p.m. on that day, October 23rd, when the die would be cast. When the greatest artillery barrage of the war to date would herald the start of a mighty conflict. It would be a 'clean' battle – no civilian destruction, no pitiful columns of helpless refugees so frequently a symbol of the twentieth century. Only the combatants would suffer. A good place to fight a war in many respects, the desert. As the hour approached in the darkness I wondered if the enemy had any inkling of what was about to descend upon them.

Brigade Headquarters was to move forward at 1.00 a.m. and was waiting a few miles to the rear of the artillery positions and was without petrol. The Royal Army Service Corps vehicles bringing a supply had not arrived. There was great anxiety because darkness had fallen and the moon was still to rise and vehicle movement at such a time was fraught with difficulty in the desert and actually locating so small a unit not easy even in daylight. The thought of Brigade Headquarters being immobile at such a crucial time was appalling. The hub of the Headquarters and of the whole Brigade of three Royal Sussex battalions was a large

29

enclosed vehicle stuffed with radio equipment and bristling with antennae, a vital vehicle the defence of which was our reason for being there. If we failed to move as a body at the appointed hour radio contact could be lost with the battalions, but as 9.40 p.m. loomed we were thinking of other matters. There was still time for the precious fuel to arrive as it just simply had to. Somehow.

A Letter from Cape Town

The Alamein front erupted exactly on time. Hundreds of gun barrels belched flame in an instant. It was an awe-inspiring sight and a frightful sound as every gun engaged in rapid fire. The Eighth Army was roaring in anger and savage defiance as a wild animal at bay turning on its pursuers. My heart thumped wildly and a cold shiver trembled through me. I felt a surge of compassion for those at the wrong end of this thunderous bombardment, a sentiment left unspoken. The ability of men to suffer massive shell fire and come up fighting was a factor we knew little of but it seemed inconceivable that anyone could survive the murderous onslaught that continued without pause into the early hours.

As we watched the tortured night sky glow and flicker while the great thunderroll thumped in our chests, each man indulged his own thoughts. History was being forged in the furnace of the moment and the lives of each of us had reached a climactic point that would never be forgotten.

Our thoughts were eventually wrested from the great drama of the night and applied to Brigade Headquarters' own personal drama. Midnight had passed almost unnoticed and there was still not a can of petrol in sight.

The staff Officers were in an agonising dilemma but within a few minutes of 1.00 a.m. as though in answer to a prayer from a high level the offending vehicles appeared and were hurriedly lined up back to back with our own transport and we rushed in to carry out a double-quick transfer job.

Petrol was always supplied in four gallon cans that were notoriously thin and were appropriately referred to as 'flimsies'. As we scrambled over the tailboards we were horrified to find the trucks running with petrol and the fumes were stifling. The cans had obviously had a rough passage and many were leaking profusely. As nailed Army boots scrambled on metal floors, the explosive potential was lethal but so urgent was haste that little heed was paid to it.

Sound cans were transferred and the remaining contents of leaking cans were hurriedly funnelled into empty vehicle tanks. Petrol was running everywhere but on the stroke of 1.00 a.m. Brigade Headquarters' column quietly slipped into gear and moved forward as if nothing had happened. In fact, nothing had and I was beginning to realise that wars can be won or lost by events that never happen, an impression that grew with experience.

The Germans, of course, handled petrol with much greater efficiency. At Alam Halfa there had been found on abandoned enemy vehicles, petrol cans that were of very robust construction and excellent design. These 'jerrycans' were looked upon as legitimate loot and were much treasured. So good were they, the 'jerrycans" virtues were sung as long and loud as those of 'Lili Marlene' and both outlived the Third Reich.

The thunder of guns intensified as we approached through the ghostly moonlight. Some colleagues were sleeping. The ability of some to sleep, come what may, never ceased to amaze me. Progress was slow and halting. Eventually we perceived that our column had reached the British minefields and there we stopped for the day. We were surrounded by a huge assembly of army units and their paraphernalia and the guns were firing and bouncing in recoil amid clouds of dust. Our aircraft seemed to monopolise the air space and there was no enemy retaliation of any sort reaching us.

Darkness fell to be relieved by the moon that seemed eager to witness the drama unfolding below it. In the very early hours movement was resumed until we reached the wire bounding another minefield. Hanging on the wire was a small triangular tin sign carrying a message full of menace. Those who were sleeping were roused and invited to read it. Beneath a representation of a skull and crossbones were inscribed the words '*ACHTUNG-MINEN*'.

At least we knew now what we were doing. We were trespassing. The congestion was nearing a state of chaos and no vehicle was moving and it was deemed wise to dig a hole for personal safety. Within a few yards of our Brigade Headquarters' vehicle – the Command Vehicle – was another belonging to a New Zealand infantry brigade also stationary in the jam of traffic. The Brigadier was moving in and out of his mobile office as we busily dug ourselves in. It was a very strange sight but a camp bed had been erected complete with blankets and, with dawn still hours away, our jaws dropped in astonishment as the Brigadier emerged clad in his pyjamas and went to bed. There was no other person who dared remove his boots and it could be fairly assumed no one else had even brought pyjamas to the Battle of El Alamein. It was an act of defiant bravery, worthy of a medal perhaps, though the citation would have made comic reading.

With the approach of dawn movement recommenced and the recumbent Brigadier had to leave his bed. Two white tapes laid on the surface marked a corridor through the minefield, a corridor cleared by the Royal Engineers beneath the cover of the artillery barrage. Just beyond the tapes the deadly mines could be partly seen where the winds had removed the sand and in the eerie dawn light they looked full of evil intent. The Engineers had erected a crude wooden sign daubed with the words 'DON'T BE A BLOODY FOOL, KEEP WITHIN THE TAPES' and no traffic sign was ever more strictly obeyed.

Overhead, shells whined all in one direction but our progress was very slow and the corridor was crowded. The glorious desert sunrise revealed a scene that would have been a prize for a Stuka party and it was obvious that things were going wrong somewhere. The traffic jam did not suggest deliberate planning. We could only wait and see rather helplessly.

Eventually we emerged from the minefield corridor and vehicles were able to fan out a little. To our astonishment we could see across our front less than a mile ahead the stern ends of a line of tanks firing their guns forward. They marked the extent of the bridgehead in the battle to occupy Miterya Ridge. They were stationary and a motley collection of practically everything was crowding up behind them. Solid armour-piercing shells from the enemy beyond were flying and ricocheting among us and we felt like sitting ducks. As we nudged slowly forward, hemmed in by artillery and their limbers, anti-aircraft guns, armoured cars, tanks, supply trucks and jeeps, we could see just ahead of us an apparently sleeping figure wrapped in a blanket, a head of curly black hair at one end and a pair of boots protruding from the other. Someone remarked on the choice of time and place for a sleep, but was corrected by someone more observant. With considerable difficulty the traffic steered reverently left or right of the solitary corpse, while great spurts of sand were suddenly erupting as the silent armour-piercing shells buried themselves in our midst. Looking down upon the motionless body, I found myself envying its peace and tranquillity. The noisy and perilous situation did not disturb the silent figure while I was fighting inwardly to contain my fears.

We stopped a few yards away and were told to dig ourselves in somewhere, anywhere, and fast. Finding some partly-filled trenches, we cleaned them out at speed wondering who may have dug them in the first place. Everything had stopped, anti-aircraft guns were manned and the tank battle ahead continued without movement. The junior officer in charge of our detachment, Lieutenant Shearer, approached and took two men to bury the mysterious corpse. The body was decomposing. Gingerly they removed the blanket and searched for identity discs. They had been removed. They found only a letter from a girl in Cape Town. With handkerchiefs around their faces, they hurriedly dug a grave alongside the body and gently rolled it in and so buried the dead soldier with his love letter.

Two pieces of plywood forming a cross and bearing the words 'UNKNOWN SOUTH AFRICAN SOLDIER' marked the spot. We could only assume he had died on patrol days before the action started. Who removed his identity discs? Who so carefully wrapped him in a blanket and left him there? Was it his friends or his enemies? His sad story was buried with him.

As the day grew older the noise intensified and the unseen flying debris from the battle increased. A truck suddenly burst into flames as it was struck. Its load of small arms ammunition and grenades exploded and flew in all directions and the fire could be said to have blown itself out. In the afternoon a cheering sight met our eyes. A small column of prisoners were being escorted from the forward area. It was accepted as a sign that perhaps something was going right somewhere though they numbered only about 40. As we gazed with undiluted joy at their approach, a Stuka suddenly snarled upon us from above. Its approach was unheard above the prevailing din and its bomb was whistling down before we could react. It exploded within yards of the column of prisoners who had reacted somewhat faster. They reassembled promptly and appeared unharmed and within a few minutes were within our midst and adding to the congestion. We assumed charge of them and there was a flurry of activity as vehicles were pressed into service to take them away.

They were all German, young, tough and well disciplined and betrayed no emotions. They waited quietly and appeared oblivious of the dangers threatening us all and were apparently unaffected by their narrow escape from injury by their own dive-bomber. Among their new guards was one Leonard Goldstein, a young Jewish tailor from north London. A good friend to us all, Leonard was short, stocky and swarthy. Like his name, he was typically Jewish and a very gentle person and very nervous. His face was a study as he stood guard over the Germans and struggled with his emotions. We all knew how Jews had been treated in pre-war Germany. What was happening to them in Germany as Leonard stood with loaded rifle in hand was only revealed at a much later time.

The necessary vehicles were assembled and the prisoners ordered to climb aboard and with a quick 'You, you and you' escorts were detailed to join them, with about 12 prisoners and one escort per truck. To his intense dismay Leonard was detailed for the final truck and the urgency of the command brooked no objections. The tailboard had already been slammed shut and secured and Leonard always had difficulty climbing over tailboards because of his lack of stature. With rifle slung over his shoulder he tried desperately to obtain a foothold and a grip on something. As he hauled himself up his rifle slipped off his shoulder, the barrel clouted him on his head, his steel helmet was dislodged and he fell off the vehicle in an undignified heap. The other vehicles were moving off as Leonard desperately tried again. As he vainly struggled a German prisoner leaned over the tailboard, relieved him of his rifle and with his other hand hauled Leonard safely aboard and with a slight bow handed him back his rifle. The truckload of prisoners lurched forward and disappeared in a cloud of dust with Leonard in charge but wishing he was somewhere else. It was the most comic episode I never laughed at. Silently I wished the prisoner well for he must have been a great character.

At the close of day 133 Infantry Brigade Headquarters departed from the scene. The whole action had been effectively stopped in its tracks by the enemy and but for the Allies' mastery of the air we would have suffered disaster. As we moved away there remained amidst all the assembled clutter of war a small area untrodden. Marked by a flimsy plywood cross, it was a spiritual oasis of peace in a harsh warring world. A sacred plot protected from desecration by a transcendent spirit that reached the souls of all who passed by. It was the resting place of an unknown soldier from South Africa, buried with a love letter and it needed no fence to protect it.

'When I Say Go'

Our journey through the moonlit night was in a northerly direction. It was a very rough ride and the shaking increased our weariness. Inevitably some stalwarts were sleeping with heads lolling and rolling in idiotic rhythm. Thinking of the past 24 hours induced a sombre mood. No senior ranks seemed able to 'put us in the picture' any more. It was plain to see that our part of the initial offensive had achieved very little. Confusion reigned up through the ranks for as far as a private could see. Only the enemy kept us informed. The little tin sign hanging on the minefield wire. The solid armour-piercing shells that ended their trajectories in our midst and the controlled demeanour of the few prisoners contained a warning, an unspoken threat. I found our journey uncomfortable in every sense.

We reached the coastal railway track that lay parallel to the road and stopped between the two in the early hours of October 26th. The road was on a small embankment that prevented any sighting of the sea beyond it. Eastwards along the tracks stood El Alamein station, solitary, useless and, under the circumstances prevailing, somewhat absurd. The thunder of artillery was well away to the westward and we were grateful for the relatively quiet peacefulness of our position. Wearily we spread around on the soft sand and, making no effort to dig any slit trenches, deeming it unnecessary, we sank rapidly into deep sleep.

The awakening was a sudden one. Flashes and explosions were suddenly erupting all around us. My immediate interpretation was that grenades were being thrown and I was paralysed by fright and confusion. It ended as quickly as it began and all I could hear was aircraft. My comrades were up and digging at high speed. Quite unable to work out in my mind what had happened and too utterly weary to bother, I ignored the whole war and returned to my slumbers.

Dawn had still not arrived when a string of heavy bombs crashed and blasted across us and I abandoned any further hope of sleep and quietly awaited the sunrise. The spreading light revealed the secrets of the first attack. The enemy aircraft had dropped 'Molotov breadbaskets' – bombs that opened up during their descent and scattered showers of small anti-personnel bombs much akin to hand grenades. Many had failed to explode in the soft sand and lay there in the morning light full of menace. We picked our way carefully until Royal Engineer bomb disposal men dealt with them.

The lessons of the night were heeded. We dug in. For six days and nights we remained between the road and the railway. Perhaps they were acting as moonlit guidelines to the enemy fliers for we suffered air attacks every day and every night of varying intensity and the indignity of constantly being driven to ground was becoming irksome. Even more irksome was the absence of information. Rumour was rife and all bad. Lurid tales of heavy casualties, of no progress being made and of situations worsening by the hour did nothing to cheer us. A much vaunted command of the air seemed dubious from our vantage point. The only firm news was, from our parochial point of view very bad. One of the Royal Sussex battalions had virtually disappeared, mainly as prisoners of war. A colonel had been killed and many others including many known to us personally. Our only casualty at Brigade Headquarters was a young man of Kent, Danny Alford, who was carried off with metal splinters in his back from one of the Molotov breadbaskets. We longed to see a London newspaper to read news of the battle but there were no deliveries.

Our inactivity was demoralising and we were pleased when early on Sunday November 1st we boarded our transport and motored across desert until we found ourselves amongst the 25-pounder guns that were as usual in full cry.

There had been a significant development in the Battle of El Alamein though we knew little of it. Australian infantry had punched a hole in the enemy line to the south of the road and were fighting their way northward to cut off a large section of the enemy infantry by gaining access to the road behind them.

To counter this dangerous situation Rommel had ordered his entire armoured forces to the north, intending to smash the Australians once and for all. There were few secrets in the desert and Montgomery noted this move with satisfaction. He planned to do the same thing and gather all his armoured divisions and engage the enemy tanks *en masse* and in his own words 'knock them for six'. His tank commanders were aghast at the plan, fearing the consequences of being 'knocked for six' themselves and suggested instead an attack further south where German and Italian infantry, denuded of tank support, held the line unaided. To break through where the line was comparatively weakly held and then swing north and west and cut off the entire enemy armoured force sounded more practical and, uncharacteristically, Montgomery acquiesced and changed the direction of the plan, codenamed 'Supercharge' accordingly. He had fixed the timing for the night of November 1st/2nd and this he did not change.

Our new surroundings were full of noise and dust. The guns were all around us and the gunners, stripped to their waists, fed their roaring, recoiling weapons of death and destruction with a precision and trained team-work that was thrilling to watch. There was little time to look around, however, for some of us were summoned to an audience of Lieutenant Shearer. A young and very earnest officer, quiet of speech and gentle in manner, he was much respected at Brigade Headquarters. He cared to a fault for the welfare of his men who referred to him when out of earshot as 'Norma'. This was not to suggest any tendency to femininity. There was none, nor was he as beautiful as the famous American film actress; it was simply good-natured irreverence, typical of the British soldier.

He spoke about Operation Supercharge and explained that ahead of our position was an enemy strong point that the Royal Sussex battalions were to overrun during the night. The maps of the desert regions, naturally, had little detail inscribed upon them. A few contour lines and little more. It was quite an achievement to get them the right way up; or round. This strong point was shown on the maps by contour lines depicting a kidney shape and so it was named Kidney Ridge. It was an insignificant geographical feature but it afforded its occupiers with a formidable field of fire. It stood in the way of 'Supercharge'.

Kidney Ridge, 'Norma' Shearer told us, could not be attacked in daylight because of its deadly field of fire, it could not be attacked in darkness because it was too difficult to find and the attacking men would lose direction so the attack would be carried out in the moonlight soon after 1.00 a.m. but the troops would still require guidance. A trail would have to be laid for them to follow and as he outlined the plan for that operation we listened in a breathless silence for the whole idea sounded highly farcical. We knew now why he was telling us so much detail. The trail-laying job was ours.

Army training manuals do not cater for every eventuality. There are occasions when improvisation is required. Our allotted task was just that in its entirety. The plan was to lay a long line of empty petrol cans from the starting point to within 200 yards of the enemy dugouts and to do it in the faint light that preceded the full moon. Every fifth can was to have five nail holes punched in one side as on dice. A lighted hurricane lamp would be inserted after cutting the top off the can. This would be placed in the line with the illuminated holes beckoning their invitation towards the British line. The final can would show, in the same way, a figure 2, to indicate 200 yards to go. There were eight of us under 'Norma' Shearer and a three-ton truck was allocated for our use. The thought of creeping around no man's land with tin cans, hurricane lamps and a three-ton truck was an enthralling one.

Hurricane lamps were Army issue – standard equipment, so they had to be carried. In the desert they were an absolute nuisance. Difficult to pack and prone to breakage, they were useless. Or had been. Lights at night could be lethal and even cigarette smokers were reduced to a 'crafty drag' so the lamps were at all times liable to be accidentally 'lost'. Fortunately we had succeeded in preserving some, so all we required was a lot of empty petrol cans. With our allotted vehicle we scoured the neighbourhood and even purloined some from the artillery area and the sweating gunners afforded us some peculiar looks. They probably thought we were on an ill-timed 'keep the desert tidy' campaign. They were far too busy to question us for they were engaged in 'blowing the living day-lights' out of the Kidney Ridge residents. We had little difficulty in assembling plenty of cans and with the required lamps duly filled and wicks trimmed, we were ready. The lamps revived memories of my childhood on a Hampshire farm, where they served as stable lamps. Memories of the delightful sound and scents as carthorses munched sweet clover hay and the flashing whites of their eyes as they looked round at the young intruder and their low muffled throaty sounds of recognition. Far off days when I dreamed of travelling in foreign lands.

All eight men under 'Norma' Shearer detailed for the midnight escapade duly assembled. We had orders to leave our rifles behind to prevent them clashing against the empty cans and only to converse in whispers and if the enemy threw up magnesium flares to remain perfectly still. There was a slight pre-moon radiance in the night sky as we climbed aboard the truck. As we moved off the cans jumped and crashed around and the din was frightful as we bumped our way towards Kidney Ridge. We crouched around the precious lamps to protect them from flying tin cans and I felt they would hear us coming in Berlin. My fears abated somewhat as I stole a backward glance through the flaps of the vehicle's tarpaulin. A long line of gun flashes marked the area we had left. A continuous thunderroll and the whine and whistle of shells filled the air. The whole world was full of noise. It was a unique experience to witness our artillery fire from the front, akin to viewing the world from outer space. As the vehicle stopped at the starting point for the tin trail, all except two jumped out and set foot on the forbidden surface of no man's land. We commenced our task immediately. The procedure was to take a can from the hands of the two men still in the truck, walk about ten paces, place it firmly down and return for another can. Perfectly simple.

It was an eerie experience. While placing the can in position the vehicle, moving slowly forward would disappear in the gloom. It was comforting to rejoin it, only to lose it again. My personal unspoken fear was of meeting an enemy patrol, its leader armed with a Luger pistol and myself armed only with a tin can. The whole episode had a farcical make-believe quality about it. It was rather awkward handling every fifth can with a lighted lamp inside it. Taking it over the tailboard, holding the can with one hand, the base of the lamp with the other and holding the illuminated side to one's chest, walking to the right and placing the crazy thing down safely without dropping it was difficult without trembling hands. It lent a wealth of new meaning to the hackneyed phrase 'carrying the can'.

As we progressed shooting started from Kidney Ridge. Tracer bullets, like high-velocity fireflies could be seen coming. They were wild and aimed at nothing in particular but an occasional close one would pass with a vicious 'snick'. This at least indicated no enemy patrols in the area. Then the dreaded flares began bursting into flickering life overhead and we froze like statues for movement is the give-away in their eerie wavering glare. We proceeded nearer to the enemy who appeared as nervous of the night as we but the flares and the rifle shots became more frequent and our progress was slow. They obviously suspected the presence of some unwelcome visitors and they could be forgiven for not knowing that a few unarmed Britishers were creeping about with tin cans. At this stage I wondered fearfully how our task would end for the three-ton truck looked enormous in the light of the flares and our eventual discovery seemed inevitable. The more we advanced the more farcical the whole idea appeared to be. Because of the flares delaying us our time was running out. The sky was heralding the imminent rising of the moon and the attack would be launched on time on the assumption that we had completed the trail and vacated the area. The mind baulked at the thought of the consequences that would otherwise befall us.

The British shells were still whining and whistling overhead and the thud and crump of their delivery could be heard in the near distance. The rifle fire was uncomfortably close to us and I realised our task was near completion when a sudden roaring flame soared up in front of us. It was a nerve-jangling fright as, just about 200 yards ahead an enemy lorry burst into flames. The cab was a mass of flames, the tyres were four rings of fire and the bed was flaming along its length. Ammunition was exploding and the whole area was bathed in glaring light. I stood and watched as Germans ran round and round throwing sand in a frantic endeavour to douche the all-revealing flames. It was a moment to relish, a vivid souvenir to retain in my memory till my dying day. Not desiring to hasten that day, I soon dashed back to the truck. The final vital illuminated sign had now been placed and the figure 2 flickered its message to whomsoever it may concern. Very keen to leave, we gathered behind the lorry tailboard to allow a quick headcount to be made. Before the lieutenant was able to do so our situation suddenly became desperate.

From a point not far in front of us a machine gun opened fire sending a continuous succession of short bursts of tracer bullets two feet from the side of the vehicle and about two feet above the surface. We stood petrified as we watched the tracers zipping past the rear wheel. A slight swing of the gun barrel to its right would end it all for us. To move the truck was out of the question. We could not dig in for we carried no tools. We could not attempt to silence the gun for we were unarmed. Its firing seemed to be on a fixed line and purely defensive and we obviously had not been seen, so we hoped the firing would stop but our luck was out.

Lieutenant Shearer swore. The first occasion I heard him desecrate the English language. He had good reason. The lamp illuminating the figure 2 had gone out and the can containing it stood several yards beyond the stream of bullets. Its replacement was absolutely essential. The attacking force would be looking for it – and soon. The young officer was confronted with a terrible dilemma. We must replace it but how? We could not go. We could not stay.

There were no options left that offered any hope and the inescapable burden of decision was his. He whispered hoarsely for a new sign to be prepared and scanned us all with anxious eyes. My heart pumped madly as I waited for him to select a candidate for suicide. To race through the bullet stream with a tin can and a lighted lamp inside it was just impossible but the impossible would have to be attempted.

'I want two volunteers,' whispered the young officer, finding himself unable to select anyone for the task.

It was a moment of truth. Two men volunteered immediately, two men who shamed the rest of us. 'Ginger' Butcher was a red-haired man from the regiment's home land. Eric Longley, a tall lean native of north-east England. Meet them in the street and the hair colour of one and the height of the other might attract a second glance. How can one man judge another?

The replacement sign was offered from the interior of the truck and 'Ginger' clutched it tightly to his chest and they both crouched by the rear wheel waiting for the order.

'When I say "go",' whispered 'Norma'.

He was counting the rounds of each burst to find the rhythm of the gunner's trigger finger to time his command to the best

51

advantage. I waited for the next moments in an agony of mind.

The order came – 'Go.'

They rushed from behind the wheel. The gunner had stopped firing. A miracle had taken place. The two ordinary young men replaced the sign and rushed back. They could have walked it. The next command was anticipated as army boots scrambled over the tailboard, the officer joined the driver, the lorry lurched forward and swung round, throwing us all to the floor. There we stayed as the rear end was presented to Kidney Ridge. There were no parting shots. Not one. We arrived back at Brigade Head-quarters safe and sound. Each one of us.

El Alamein and Points West

Reunited with our personal weapons, we each dug, or found, a slit trench to sleep in. The whole area vibrated with the con-cussion of artillery and with loose sand sifting into the trench and gently burying me I fell into a deep slumber thinking of miracles, of two men defying a machine gun that stopped firing, of a brigadier who went to bed in his pyjamas. Valour, like beauty, is in the eye of the beholder.

After almost two hours' sleep amid the thunderous roar of the 25-pounders I was wakened by the quiet voice of 'Norma' Shearer. He was saying something about prisoners. After crawling out of the trench and shaking the sand off like an old dog emerging from a river, I proceeded to a circular area surrounded by vehicles, stacks of stores and sundry clutter. It had been hastily designated as a reception centre for prisoners, some of whom were on their way. While we had soundly slept, the men of the Royal Sussex had found their way to Kidney Ridge and had gone right in and carried out the dirty work, the First World War rifle and bayonet and grenade-type dirty work. The defenders had been 'winkled out' and we awaited the first contingent.

The Medical Officer was installing his first-aid post – a trestle table and a hessian screen – in readiness on the fringe of the half-acre site. The first light of dawn's eternal promise was visible when two small groups of strangers were seen approaching with a solitary escort. They were Italians and Germans, allies but apart. Oil and water. They were escorted by a former colleague, one Charlie Baker, who looked at his feet as he replied to my enquiry about events on Kidney Ridge.

'My God! It was awful,' he said. 'Some of them hid in underground bunkers and refused to come out.'

Several times he repeated to me how they were ordered to emerge and surrender but refused. He then quietly related how they found petrol stacked there and threw some cans in the bunkers followed by grenades.

'It was terrible,' he said, 'but they would not come out. We yelled at them but they just would not surrender.'

He was desperately trying to justify an action taken in the terrible turmoil of hand-to-hand fighting. There was no need for him to do so. Except to himself.

Most of the prisoners appeared to be suffering from wounds of varying severity. With one exception they had walked in unaided but ripped clothing and blood dripping from finger tips were evidence of their plight. One young German had hobbled in assisted by two of his colleagues. He sat on a box and stared into space while his countrymen stood in a group and conversed quietly. The Italians were perhaps more practical and wanted to be friends. The war was over for them and they did not disguise their pleasure. They craved food, water and medical attention. They huddled round the first-aid post and a queue had to be enforced. The Germans asked no favours. As the dawn light heightened the scream of a lone Stuka was heard above the gunfire. The bomb whistled its approach and exploded with a great flash 50 yards away. Crawling out from under the nearest truck, I was horrified to find the prisoner-of-war area empty but to my relief the inmates all re-appeared from various hiding places. Perhaps there was something about prisoners that attracted Stukas.

Feeling concerned for the young German who had to be assisted in, I approached him as he sat in solitary silence. His left trouser leg had been reduced to a blood-soaked tattered rag sticking to his thigh from which blood seeped down his bare leg, into and over his boot and stained the sand. Before I could indicate to him that he should seek medical aid he turned his head and our eyes met.

His face was boyish in its youthfulness but it radiated absolute venom. His cold blue eyes stared fixedly at me and his countenance dared me to offer him help. The vision of hate and utter loathing left me in a state of bewilderment as though a friend had hurled an insult. Anger rose within me and I could not face his awful stare. As he had obviously chosen to bleed to death rather than seek help from any of us, I caught the glances of his older compatriots who had assisted him previously and indicated the medical queue. Promptly they took an arm each round their shoulders and, ignoring his weak protests, they dragged him to the front of the line. As he lurched past me I noticed the inscription on the buckle of his tunic belt. *'Gott Mitt Uns'* – 'God with us'. He disappeared from my view for ever behind the hessian screen leaving me with a disturbing sense of grievous insult. I assumed such arrogance could only indicate he was an indoctrinated specimen of the Hitler Youth Movement. Medical attention would heal his damaged leg but his mentors had inflicted far more grievous harm than his enemies.

More prisoners trudged wearily in as the morning progressed and it was gratifying to assemble the enemy in defeat. Enthralling too to find the occasional German with a command of the English language and an inclination to use it. One predicted we would be blown right out of Egypt eventually and if they had had as much artillery it would have happened long ago. He inferred we were not being quite fair. Another had studied English in readiness for the occupation of the United Kingdom and with a shrug of his shoulders agreed it would be useful in his new status as a prisoner of war.

Later that day, happily deficient in hurricane lamps, Brigade Headquarters moved to a new location a short distance north. The track in front of our vehicle erupted as shells burst in rapid succession. It was a new experience for us and no one spoke as we motored steadily on. The shell bursts were scattered and occasional and revealed the characteristics of the notorious 88-millimetre gun originally designed as an anti-aircraft weapon but used very effectively as a field gun. Its rapid fire rate made it a much feared artillery piece.

As we came to a halt we immediately formed a defensive arc ahead of the command vehicle and dug ourselves in at great speed as shells continued to whine overhead and burst beyond us or to the left or right of us and in front of us conveying a nasty impression they were trying to get our range. A wind was raising the sand and our forward vision was limited by the resultant dust cloud out of which the 88s were homing in. Guns behind us were sending shells whistling in the opposite direction and we dug in as never before and were grateful for soft sand.

The shellfire could only be described as light and intermittent and I shuddered at the prospect of a real bombardment. At least the Stuka pilots gave warning of their intentions. We felt we had the measure of their brand of beastliness and preferred it to the vicious shell bursts that were un-announced and unpredictable. The Brigade Headquarters' sergeant major made a hurried tour of inspection and enquired if we were as scared as he was which made us feel better. He was followed by another visitor who moved from trench to trench in a crouching run, stopping frequently to lay flat as shells whined overhead. He was in charge of mail and was on his rounds. A letter from home under shellfire was a great moment. The Army Post Office always delivers, we were assured by a very brave postman.

The darkness laid a blanket of peace on the uncomfortable scene but the night was spent in considerable anxiety. The ever-present fear that things were going wrong because no one ever said they were going right was prominent that night. Why was the Command Vehicle being risked under shell-fire? There was a nasty suspicion abroad that either the Brigade Headquarters or the 88-millimetre guns were not supposed to be there.

Came the dawn and news of our imminent departure. A hasty desert breakfast and a hurried loading of men and materials and we departed eastward and returned to the same spot near El Alamein station where we had spent six days dodging the attentions of bombers. We immediately ran across the road to the shore of the glittering blue sea and enjoyed the luxury of a prolonged dip in the briny, each with one eye on the sky.

Then we were given news that depressed

us beyond belief. As the Brigade had lost virtually one battalion and was consequently as out of balance as a two-legged milking stool, we were being withdrawn from the battle and next morning we would return to the Nile valley for reinforcement and re-training as a brigade. It was news ill-received. After eleven days of the battle we were no longer any use. We were to leave it all to everyone else. We were to withdraw to safety, to easier living, to better food, to the bright lights and carnal delights of Alexandria and our disappointment was bitter. Such was the spirit of the Eighth Army and the lure of the desert. To leave it was the action of deserters. In spite of the military logic of the decision we were insulted by it. To have a new battalion fresh out from the United Kingdom grafted on to us, men who had not even got their knees brown, to start serious training all over again was a bitter pill to swallow. The outcome of the battle was still, as far as we knew, undecided. We still retained our faith in victory. Only the timing was at issue and we could well miss the defeat of the Afrika Korps and that would be grossly unfair.

We retired for the night simmering with discontent. There were those who declared they would apply for transfers to other units still in the battle. The majority, myself included, decided come what may we would stay with 133 Brigade and with our friends even if transfers were permitted. A new and restored brigade up to full strength could rejoin the desert war at a later date or it could be despatched almost anywhere. However the issue was argued, the bitterness remained and only sleep ended it.

Next morning, November 4th, after another quick breakfast we packed ourselves aboard our transport which was lined up in readiness to climb on to the road and turn right for Alexandria. There was a delay. We sat there like holidaymakers in a traffic jam. There was little conversation. No one wished to see the gracious sweep of the Nile or the luscious green of the valley with its date palms and its irrigated crops or the water buffalo or the donkeys or the cafes and bars of Alexandria with its teeming crowds. No small boys heading for boarding school were ever more reluctant.

After a prolonged and tedious wait with no explanations offered the column moved off, climbed on to the road and turned – left. We looked at each other in astonishment. What was going on? There was no way of finding out but the truth would reveal itself if we continued riding to the west.

Leaving the road and proceeding across the desert we were astounded to see other columns romping across the sand in the same direction on both sides. There was a great waving of arms and ribald cheering. The truth was revealing itself but it was almost unbelievable. We were afraid to utter the obvious in case we were dreaming.

The vehicle columns were growing closer together and they were an astonishing mixture as different arms became intermingled. Suddenly our doubts were dispelled. We were passing wrecked and burning tanks and they were German. We crowded the tailboard and surveyed a scene that was absolutely chaotic and completely intoxicating. In the centre of the careering columns of vehicles of every military description stood a solitary Redcap, a Military Policeman trying vainly to keep some order in the traffic flow and being completely ignored.

As we passed him he held his hat high in the air and yelled to us, 'We've got the b–s this time!'

It was victory and the exhilaration was tremendous. The carnage was incredible. Enemy equipment was lying everywhere. German tanks, half-track personnel carriers and trucks smashed and burning. Many of the enemy tanks still contained ammunition and were exploding in all directions. Some contained dead crew members in their flaming interiors and even that smell did not deter our soaring spirits. Our communal cup of joy was brimming over. It was heady stuff and we were drunk with elation. A few

Stukas appeared from somewhere and were presented with a huge target that could hardly be missed. From their vantage point the scene must have been memorable indeed as a floodtide of men and materials flowed over and around the scattered remnants of a defeated Army. Unfortunately for them, their massive target possessed a correspondingly massive fire power and everyone who could fired everything they had with a gay abandon that bordered on the hilarious. They departed in haste.

We passed within feet of the 75-millimetre gun barrel of a burning *panzer-wagen* with a dead crew member sprawled on his back beside it. His clothing was charred and blackened by fire and two vacant eyes stared through a black crawling mask of flies. The scene symbolised so many aspects of the day. The broken myth of the invincibility of the Afrika Korps. The inevitable defeat of the Third Reich. The basic sin, futility and waste of war. The real winners were the flies. There were pathetic little mounds where the enemy had found time to bury their dead, each marked symbolically with a rifle and bayonet upended and stuck in the sand, often with a battered steel helmet hung on the rifle butt or even a steering wheel and its column – anything that came easily to hand.

We dug in for the night in soft sand and thought back over the most fantastic day of our lives. We had expected to be near Alexandria but the historic turn of the tide had swept us along with it and we rejoiced. Deep within all was the great satisfaction of knowing that wonderful news would be sweeping across the United Kingdom and cheering the hearts of our families and all those good people slogging away on farms and in factories to make such events possible. The church bells rang merrily over the shires of Britain and their joyful peals stirred an echo among the desert carnage.

There was to be a dawn start for us for we were to make a fast move to place ourselves behind the enemy base of El Daba, to apprehend any of them attempting to pull out and join the rout. To accomplish this we travelled in a deep southerly arc and immediately encountered hundreds of Italians trudging eastwards. The Germans appeared to have fled in everything on wheels and their Italian allies were stranded. They were vainly seeking someone who would stop long enough to be surrendered to but we did not want them. They called out for water but we could spare them none. There was not time to offer them succour of any kind. We pointed to the east and bid them walk on. The more miles we travelled the more sad groups we encountered and the greater their helplessness. Someone would round them up we hoped for it gave us no pleasure to leave them to their fate in the vast thirsty wilderness.

The surface was good and we travelled fast until the light truck I shared with five others coughed, spluttered and died. The rest of the column continued on its way and soon disappeared and we were entirely alone with nothing to guide us but the wheel tracks leading away into infinity. A slight breeze was gradually smoothing them out of existence. Ted Lightfoot, the driver, cursed volubly and grabbed his tool kit, lifted the bonnet and commenced disconnecting the fuel pipes having diagnosed a blockage therein. In the event of a breakdown the standing order was to remain by the vehicle and await help to be sent back. Driver Ted had been in this predicament on a former occasion and waited three days for rescue and it was not an ordeal he wished to suffer again. So he blew down the offending fuel pipes with all his lung-power and dismantled the carburettor and re-assembled it all very carefully. With our fingers crossed in support, he coaxed the motor back to life and we anxiously followed the fading wheel tracks. Our dilemma intensified when we came upon diverging tracks. There followed an anxious discussion heightened by nervous tension to a heated argument. Do we follow the right-hand or the left-hand track? both of which were barely discernable. In the event the left-hand track was followed but the argument simmered on. We had no idea where our friends were likely to stop and if our choice was a wrong one they would be unlikely ever to find us in a rescue attempt. Our fears increased by the mile. Though we carried water and reserve rations we were little better off than the hapless Italians we had met earlier. Eventually a large sand dune hove into view ahead of us and halfway up its smooth golden face stood a small armoured scout car. Lying on their stomachs peering over the razor-edged crest with binoculars were two bush-hatted Australians. The situation was self-explanatory.

As we approached the two men scrambled back from the summit on their stomachs then got to their feet and ran down to meet us gesticulating wildly. We met them by their scout car where the tracks we had followed terminated.

'Where in hell do you think you're going?' we were asked by one, a sergeant.

'We are looking for 133 Brigade,' we explained rather lamely.

'And who the devil are they?' he demanded, not expecting a reply or getting one. 'If you go over that ridge in that b—y truck you will be blown off the face of the earth,' he said very meaningfully.

We were lost completely, even for words.

'Why don't you just turn around and get

to hell away from here while you are able,'
he kindly advised us.

This we promptly did amid a chorus of 'I
told you so,' from some and an unhappy
silence from others.

There was only one option left for us, to
travel north and hope to find a friendly face
to take us in rather than an unfriendly one
we so nearly encountered.

Light was failing rapidly and Ted Lightfoot drove as fast as he dared and when
gathering darkness had all but extinguished
our hopes of salvation we spotted stationary
army vehicles ahead and as we drew near we
were astonished to see 'Norma' Shearer
coming to meet us. We could hardly believe
our good fortune.

'I was worried about you all,' said he.
'Congratulations on getting here safely. Did
you have any trouble finding us?'

'No, Sir,' came the reply. 'No trouble at
all, Sir.'

We joined our comrades who were dug in
and facing north-east towards high ground
on which stood El Daba now shrouded in
darkness. It was an anxious and eerie night
with little sleep as we peered through the
gloom for signs of movement on our front.
None came for the Germans had left before
we arrived. It was one of their rearguards
the Australians had saved us from and the
Italians were only seeking salvation which

could wait till daylight. The daylight came and Italians with it in their hundreds. It was impossible for us to do more than shepherd them together like stray flocks of sheep. There was neither food nor water for such a multitude. No loaves or fishes. Many of them carried emergency rations and some water and there was little prospect of them enjoying anything else that day.

They all carried on their persons large quantities of personal letters and documents which they proceeded to tear up and throw away. There were propaganda postcards depicting a German and an Italian soldier with a hand each on the collar of a British 'Tommy' on his knees. They tore those up too. They were eventually removed from our care to await transport elsewhere and we were left with an acreage of desert littered with waste paper. Forming a long line, we moved across the area and picked it all up and burned it because the British Army never leaves a mess behind it. Cleaning up an empty desert behind a defeated army evoked some muttered protests but we moved away leaving the scene as clean and tidy as any wandering Arab could hope to find it.

Reaching the coastal road, we moved across it and stopped for the day. It was a day of heavy rain. The desert soon became impossible to drive on as wheeled traffic soon bogged down. The temperature dropped sharply and we were distinctly uncomfortable in our light khaki drill. Evidence of Italian occupation abounded in this area. Many of their tanks, small and primitive, were standing around with no sign of damage, having presumably succumbed to mechanical problems. A line of trenches were found with discarded letters, postcards and empty Chianti bottles and small red hand grenades scattered around. Known as egg grenades, we were warned not to touch them and we picked our way with care. A mound of sand concealed the bodies of two of their dead. The whole scene was an unsavoury mess and we expected to be ordered to tidy it up. But for the little red eggs we probably would have been.

The next morning we moved onto the coast road and headed west. Traffic travelled bumper to bumper as far as the eye could see. Every arm of every service in the desert war was in an incredible mix-up and every driver was trying to keep up with his own unit. In desperation some would drive on the wrong side of the road as so little traffic was moving east, only to be ordered off the road by the Military Police to take their chance on the sand, where, because of the rain, they immediately sank to their axles. British, Australian, New Zealanders, South African, Free French and Indians, all in utter confusion, pushed slowly on and everyone was happy.

On high ground ahead lay Fuka airfield, the starting point for the dive-bombers that gave us a rough time on Alam Halfa. An Italian Fiat bi-plane was standing on its nose near the road and a dead Italian soldier lay on the wet sand with his head two feet from a puddle in the road. Every right-hand wheel of hundreds of vehicles sloshed dirty water over his face and into his open mouth.

There were many wrecked and burned vehicles littered alongside the road where they had vainly attempted to escape the attentions of the Royal Air Force. Each wreck was stark evidence of the countless desperate dramas that had been played out along that narrow road. There was a small railway station blown to pieces and the largest piece of masonry was a headstone emblazoned with a list of German names in elaborate Gothic script, marking a communal grave. We pulled off the road for the night and arrived in Mersa Matruh the following morning. The little township looked quite beautiful as we looked down upon it from high ground. Date palms and shrubbery and a clear blue little bay that sparkled in the sunshine was a sight for desert-weary eyes. The enemy had left the day before.

Mersa Matruh had been a peacetime

station for the British Army and at the eastern end of the town was an immaculate little cemetery dating back to those days on the orderly crosses that still maintained their lonely silent vigil. New enemy graves had been added to the sad ranks and one could believe the Germans had tidied all the little mounds and cut the grass before leaving. After the death and destruction of the previous days, this peaceful scene carried a message of hope for mankind.

The whole area around Mersa Matruh was littered with abandoned enemy material of all descriptions. There was a tremendous stockpile of aircraft bombs spaced out over acres of ground and we could only breathe sighs of relief that they had not been used. We remained in the area for 12 days assembling enemy stores and swimming in the bay but we had an uncomfortable spell of cold wet weather and a sandstorm that blew for two days. The desert pursuit had left us stranded. We knew without being told that 133 Infantry Brigade would be moving back to the Nile Valley. Meanwhile the, by now, immortalised Eighth Army pursued its old enemy hundreds of miles towards Tunisia where Operation Torch, the landings in North Africa, sealed the fate of the Afrika Korps and eventually cleared the enemy from the whole continent, as predicted by General Montgomery.

A church parade was organised on Sunday November 15th. A 15-hundredweight truck was pressed into use for a pulpit and the Royal Sussex Padre, Captain the Reverend Pritchard M.C. delivered an impassioned and unforgettable sermon.

'Every man of you,' he averred, 'at some time in the past few weeks has experienced religious feelings, even if you never have before. So you all know who to thank for your life.

'Thank God,' he called, 'that you are still alive. Do not thank your officers or your N.C.O.s, it was nothing to do with them. Thank God.'

To which his little congregation, standing with bare heads bowed gave the only appropriate reply, 'Amen.'

We spent Christmas amid the palm trees of Sidi Bishr camp on the outskirts of Alexandria. 133 Brigade was never made up to strength. It was disbanded. Brigade Headquarters' staff were returned to their respective battalions and the Royal Sussex became part of an Indian Division. We trained with the Rajputana Rifles and the Sikhs and prepared for the next stage of our foreign service. We were destined to join the Persia and Iraq force.

Exodus

The news of our new role caused a ripple of excitement throughout the battalion. The Persia and Iraq force known as Paiforce operated in a huge area. It would mean extensive travel and we had acquired a nomadic instinct. Ever since returning from Mersa Matruh in November we had been 'stooging' around the fringes of the Nile Valley and we were more than a little bored for it was now March 1943. Our first move was to be to Baghdad and that was approximately 1,000 miles away.

Persia, or by its modern name, Iran, and Iraq were of crucial importance to the Allied cause. It was territory the Afrika Korps would have raced through to meet their countrymen in Russia, driving south through the Caucasus if they had not been defeated at El Alamein. Oil flowed through pipelines in Iraq to the Mediterranean port of Haifa and in Iran were the great oilfields in the south pumping oil into tankers in the Shatt El Arab.

The Germans had waxed influential in Iran with a civilian army of technical experts paving the way for their armies until the

British and the Russians both invaded the country in 1941, meeting each other just north of Teheran. Then the importance of Iran was heightened by the organisation of a supply route for American war material to Russia, that was shipped to the Persian Gulf and carried by rail and road 800 miles across Iran to the Red Army.

To reach Baghdad entailed crossing the Sinai desert into Palestine, over the River Jordan into Trans-Jordan and across the vast empty wastelands to the Iraqi capital. On March 9th we journeyed around Ismailia, across the Suez Canal and stopped for the night, before setting forth across the Sinai. It was 100 miles to Palestine and for much of the distance we travelled through a 'picture-book' desert with huge sand dunes gracefully moulded and sculpted by winds, with high golden crests clashing with a clear blue sky. Fringes of sand blowing over the high ridges revealed how these colossal tonnages of sand moved across the landscape. Egyptian workers were engaged in an endless task removing sand from the road surface as our convoy pursued its course out of Egypt.

To undertake the Sinai crossing is to feel the presence of biblical history. Moses, Aaron and Abraham and the ancient tribes of Israel on their way to the Promised Land trod this vast wilderness which would have appeared the same then as now. Their achievements in making such epic journeys could be appreciated and wondered at. Modern man is often humbled by the history of his ancient forebears as the Pyramids of Gizeh dwarf the twenty-first-century tourist.

Passing into Old Testament Palestine, we rumbled through the ancient town of Beersheba. Like the Sinai itself, it had probably changed little since biblical times, but the presence of history is felt rather than seen.

Army convoys travelled slowly covering an average 120 miles daily and we threaded our way thus through rocky hills on a road with nerve-wracking bends and unguarded precipices into the richer lands of orange groves, with beautiful scenery and rural abundance. Our eyes had been starved of such colour. It was a new world and we felt reborn. With one day devoted to vehicle maintenance, we journeyed on to the West Bank area of harsh stony soil and barren hillsides tilled by Arabs using primitive wooden ploughs pulled by a camel or bullock to scrape what must have been a frugal living for man and beast.

Crossing the River Jordan, which looked surprisingly small, we commenced the long climb up to sea level and on up for miles by a twisting tortuous road into the Kingdom of Jordan. There was still 500 miles of travel to reach Baghdad. Crossing a huge grassy plain and motoring non-stop through hilly Amman, in the early hours we passed through an area covered in black volcanic rocks that covered the landscape for miles. Alongside the road was the buried Haifa pipeline accompanied by telegraph poles in a perfectly straight line that stretched seemingly into eternity. The occasional pumping station was graced with a number and we spent a night at H.4, Haifa Four, and a more lonely outpost of man's endeavour would be hard to find. To travel alongside the Haifa pipeline was to marvel at the ingenuity of modern man whose appetite for oil drives him to lay a pipeline across hundreds of miles of hot and barren desert. For it was hot and barren all the way to Baghdad, with lonely Rutbah the only sizeable habitation on the route. There were herds of camels that seemed to graze the bare earth and not a sight of water till we crossed the Euphrates river and approached our destination, Baghdad.

Viewing the ancient city from afar revived school-day impressions of romantic Arabia. Cupolas and minarets dominated the skyline over a vast sprawling metropolis that appeared to have grown out of the desert. Soon after settling in under canvas on the outskirts of Baghdad we were deluged by heavy thunderstorms and the camp became a morass of sticky clinging mud, making life uncomfortably cold. Each night the camp was besieged by packs of wild dogs who maintained a persistent chorus of plaintive howls and from a nearby backwater issued another chorus from hordes of frogs. The dogs – pariahs or pi-dogs – would sneak into the camp in the stygian gloom of the early hours to raid the cook-house dustbins, giving those of us on guard duty nasty frights as the lids fell with a clatter. Our romantic notions of old Baghdad were dying fast.

We were soon let loose in the old city, an easy walking distance away over the King Faisal bridge that spanned the River Tigris. A murky, fast-flowing torrent after the rains, the Tigris was anything but inviting. The streets were peopled by a teeming multitude and the whole city wore a cloak of dusty antiquity. In the bazaars one felt the pulse of Arab commercial life with endless bargaining and haggling for wares on display ranging from melons, dates, corn and spices to cottons, silks, carpets and skins and pots and pans. I stared in disbelief at the sight of a brand-new upright Raleigh bicycle from Nottingham and have wondered ever since how it ever arrived there. The banging and clashing of coppersmiths shaping their plates and dishes among all the general din and hubbub combined to leave a lasting impression on all who entered the bazaars of Baghdad. Emerging into the streets where camels were common traffic, my mind recalled schoolday stories of rich Arab merchants making epic journeys across empty deserts with their camel trains laden with goods to sell. Now it all had acquired a new and noisy reality for little had changed.

Our stay was confined to two weeks. The camp was not a comfortable one and we were glad to leave it, for the mud had never completely dried. The new destination was Khanaqin, a town to the north of Baghdad in the ancient region of Kurdestan, now divided between Iraq and Iran, wherein dwelt the Kurds, a tribal nation now without a home of its own. The journey was by train in enclosed box wagons and it could not have been less comfortable if the train had run on square wheels. 16 to a wagon, we could lie down, sardine fashion, but every rail joint jolted our hip bones. The journey was very slow, it started at 1.00 a.m., lasted nine hours and was the most undignified journey we ever suffered.

Khanaqin, a mud-hutted Arab town set among date palms, was a picture of Middle Eastern tranquillity, teeming with dogs and bare-footed children who watched us march through their dusty street while the women-folk ran for cover and the menfolk ignored us. North of the town was a region of low rolling hills covered in green grass and flowers and sheltered dry river beds or wadis. Eight miles beyond Khanaqin we moved off the road and searched for a camp site. The grass was soft and inviting but was the home for a multitude of large black ants that had worn bare tracks in the grass and could be observed marching back and forth with great resolution. We chose a dry gravel-strewn wadi and set up the 180-pounders, the standard army tent of the day.

I found the view to the north quite irresistible. The huge Zagros mountain range shut out the rest of the world. Massive snow-capped peaks and crags and valleys glowing purple in the distance with mysterious black shadows and glistening white summits as they stood immense and dramatic in the sunshine were a challenge and an invitation to all who gazed upon them. Beyond that mighty barrier lay the ancient Kingdom of Persia whose great civilisation and military conquests of bygone ages wrote an indelible page in the history of mankind. I secretly longed to answer the impelling invitation of the mountains and travel in the company of those magnificent peaks. It was a wish that was granted and soon.

One Royal Sussex battalion had earlier passed among the peaks into Iran but the circumstance that fulfilled my yearning was a novel one. I was a member of a small party summoned before our company commander who informed us we were to be temporarily attached to the Corps of Military Police who were under strength and we would serve with them until they could be reinforced from the United Kingdom and in a few days we were to leave the battalion and proceed to Teheran to carry out our duty.

In spite of some misgivings about becoming a military policeman, I was excited beyond words at the prospect of a 500-mile lorry ride to Teheran, through those fabulous mountains and on to new scenes in a new land and indeed a new life. There were many of our fellows who envied us this escape from battalion life and there were those who accused us of 'going over to the enemy' by joining the Military Police.

The dry wadi had been our home for 20 days when Mother Nature taught us a lesson. There came a violent thunderstorm and heavy rain. Thunder rumbled and echoed around the grassy hills and the distant mountains were lost behind a grey curtain of sheeting rain. A trickle of water appeared in the river bed and within a few minutes it grew to a raging torrent. Water swept through the tents like a flood tide. Personal belongings floated away never to be seen again. The cookhouse was knee-deep in a swirling whirlpool and many tents collapsed as pegs pulled out of softened earth and we were plunged into misery. It was never quite understood why the disaster was not foreseen. With hindsight it was realised that camping in a river bed was hardly wise, but it seemed a good idea at the time. We were learning the hard way.

The camp was still in a mess two days after the downpour when, on April 27th the Teheran party left in two 15-hundredweight trucks under Lieutenant Hardy and Sergeant Lawrence. The journey took us across a flat barren plain that was burning hot where a few Bedouins with their goats and sheep and goatskin tents somehow obtained a living from its unfriendly soil. The mountains towered over us as we approached the Pai-tak Pass where the rough dusty road twisted and writhed its way along a narrow ledge with a frightening drop on our right side with wreckage of vehicles strewn down its lower slopes. The higher we climbed the more hair-raising the view and we fervently hoped we would not encounter some Arab trader's battered old lorry hurtling downhill on its way to Baghdad. With a final backward glance at the shimmering Iraqi plain, we moved through the mountains of Iran. We spent the night in a lonely hut with a walled courtyard surrounded by silent brooding peaks wondering, if the walls could speak, what travellers' tales they could tell.

The following morning we journeyed through our first Iranian town, Kermanshah and found the Royal Sussex battalion that had preceded us into Iran camped beyond it on a flat plain with a solitary mountain behind them with snow on its peak. We had dinner with them and stayed for the remainder of the day. It was a picturesque situation with cultivated crops on one side of the very hot plain and the lonesome mountain on the other side with its cap of snow glittering in the sunshine. Before the day was over the sun was lost behind thunder clouds and heavy rain reduced the camp to a quagmire. We left them early next morning and we seemed fated to leave every camp site a sea of mud. The Iranian roads were rough and after 20 miles we limped back to the battalion camp with broken springs and with a different vehicle set off again to travel over 100 miles to Malayer.

The following day the journey was a memorable one. The long dusty road drew alongside the Iranian Railway. Here at last was the physical reality of the American supply route to Russia. A lonely flat barren expanse unchanged in centuries cut through by the iron rails of modernity and to our joy, coming as though to a pre-arranged tryst, was a magnificent old American steam loco-motive lugging a long heavy train of goods wagons. Its funnel was belching great clouds of black smoke and steam issued from every joint as it laboured its way north. As it neared the spot where road and rail met we disembarked and watched its approach. The American driver leaned out of his cab and upon seeing us he waved with one hand and pulled the whistle cord with the other. It was a great moment in that empty waste-land as the old engine gave voice to the fascinating moaning whistle so beloved by train enthusiasts. It lumbered by within feet of us with the driver waving his enthusiastic greeting and the undulating moan of the whistle answering our cheers and waving arms. We all felt a wave of emotion at this symbolic cameo picture of a great international war effort in action hundreds of miles from the war itself in a remote region few people in the Western world knew of or heeded.

As we wended our way across the desert waste we could see, miles ahead, the huge golden dome of the great mosque of the holy Islamic city of Qum. As we stopped in the streets, curious crowds thronged round our vehicles. The degree of disease, hunger and squalid poverty that was evident dismayed us. Hands were outstretched for anything we cared to throw and one starving couple with a scrawny sunburnt little infant of few days offered us the child for ten rials which at that time was equivalent to two shillings. We were pleased to move away from the crowd to the comparatively luxurious railway station where we spent the night on the waiting room floor.

Driving north from Qum, the heat was oppressive and the road was thick with powdery dust. It was a region of desert, mountains and dry salt lakes. The great salt pans were so dazzling in the relentless sun, it was difficult to gaze upon them. After 90 miles of this sun-baked wilderness we could see miles ahead the huge mass of snow-capped mountains of the Elburz range. Beneath them stood the sprawling city of Teheran. As we entered the city on May 1st it was thronging with the Russian Army celebrating the communist Labour Day and I felt we had landed on another planet.

Where the Flies Die

Teheran was a young city by Eastern standards and visually dominated by the Elburz mountains a few miles north. They formed a tremendous and strikingly beautiful backcloth to the bustling city. Covered by the winter snows they are gradually revealed in their rugged grandeur as the snowline rises with the onset of summer temperatures. The dominating feature is the volcanic cone of Mount Demavend that soars to 18,700 feet and never loses its cap of snow. The melting snows formed the water supply for Teheran and were channelled to the city streets through hand-hewn tunnels across the intervening wasteland. The water flowed along street gutters and provided a supply for most of the population. Donkeys and horses drank from the gutters, women did their household washing in them and beggars soothed their sore and aching feet in the chilly water. There was an air of decay in Teheran though modern shops abounded in the main avenues – Ferdowsi, Lalezar and Shah Riza, the great wide thoroughfare bisecting the city. Cinemas and restaurants were well patronised and horse-drawn droshkis and modern motor cars intermingled in the streets being driven with the reckless abandon common to Eastern traffic. Poverty, disease and blindness, wealth, luxury and opulence, the old and the new, the good and the bad, a walk in the city avenues revealed it all.

Teheran had beautiful wares to display, historic ceramic art, metal work and traditional Persian carpets of awe-inspiring workmanship. It also had ugly warts on its countenance, decadence, sickness and starvation, corruption and crime and dirt.

For a city so many miles from any theatre of war, it had an uncommon number of troops in its streets. Russians armed to the teeth, American servicemen of Railroad Operating Companies, seemingly with a jeep each, Indian soldiers from our own division, Rajputs and Sikhs, British soldiers and the Iranian Army whose officers were attired like dandies and other ranks shabby and dishevelled giving an impression their paymasters had adhesive fingers.

Foreign embassies clustered near the city centre and horse-drawn water carts were a common sight emerging from the British Embassy where it was rcputed the only source of fresh spring water existed. Medical services did not seem to exist in Teheran and I have memories of a dead horse lying in a street on its back with distended belly and four rigid legs testifying to the number of days since it died.

We soon settled into our police duties finding them varied and interesting. Teheran was a leave centre for British troops, though not highly rated among the rank and file. Leave entitlement was always a problem for the Persia and Iraq Force because of the vast distances from any town to the next. The most attractive centres for a soldier's holiday were Beirut and the Holy Land but this was not possible for many until a later date and very few in fact ever enjoyed their full allotted span of leave on their foreign service. Those who came to Teheran had endured a rugged journey of many miles and faced the same on their return and the Military Police had no desire to spoil their brief and well-earned holidays. Sailors from the Gulf were occasionally seen and as the Royal Navy had no Shore Patrols six hundred miles from the sea, the Military Police kept a watchful and authorised eye on them. Routine street patrols were usually uneventful except for a free meal in any restaurant of choice, for the proprietors were at great pains to humour the Redcaps who could place their establishments out of bounds at the stroke of a pen. It smacked slightly of blackmail but it was the custom.

Prostitution and its attendant ills were rife in Teheran. Any attack of venereal disease was referred to as 'a Persian cold' and police patrols in out-of-bounds areas of the city were frequent. Any British serviceman apprehended in the red light districts was returned to his unit without argument. The vice patrols included house searches and the first I was engaged in set the pattern for many and was a revealing insight into the Eastern way of life. The house was typical of many, two-storeyed, open-fronted and flat-roofed, it faced a little courtyard sur-rounded by a high wall with access through a wooden door. The Redcap corporal opened the door without knocking and we stepped into the courtyard uninvited. The lady of the house was seated on cushions engaged in some domestic needlecraft. Her spouse was plucking at a stringed musical instrument and their daughter was singing. Eastern music may sound strange to Western ears but in its home setting its plaintive beauty and purity of tone is enchanting. We rudely invaded this delightful domestic scene and searched around the house in an outrageous violation of privacy by Western standards and left without a word being spoken or one melodious note being lost. We had been completely ignored, an experience I found disturbing every time it occurred.

A surprising feature of Teheran was its role as host to refugees from Poland. Camps had been established outside the city and were on the list of police patrols for they, too, were out of bounds to British servicemen. They provided a lesson in the art of survival. Many of the refugees were aged and they had all endured the loss of their homes and possessions and a long rough journey to Teheran. Families had been dispersed with little hope of any reunions. One camp of tents erected among pomegranate trees typified the stoic nature of the Poles. They had organised a camp laundry service, a communal kitchen and an open-air theatre.

Some Polish girls found employment in Teheran shops and some drifted into prostitution. Considering the blight of hopelessness on the life of any youthful refugee, a merciful view may be taken of prostitution but such girls were not welcome in the camps and were condemned to drift, homeless, in a foreign land. The casualties of war and its many upheavals are legion and not all are included in official statistics.

Contrary to a widely held belief, the Redcaps were the common soldier's good friends. Errant American G.I.s received far rougher treatment from their service police. They were bundled off and 'slammed in the cooler' with little respect for their dignity. At the first sign of too much beer or vodka with his restaurant dinner the hapless American felt a hand on his collar and his meal was left unfinished.

On the northern outskirts of Teheran stood a new, German-built hospital used by the British Army and staffed by army nurses. It drew its military patients from a huge area. An adjacent convalescent-cum-transit camp was also a security responsibility for the Military Police and it provided us with many opportunities to visit our Royal Sussex friends who through illness or accident found themselves alone in the world.

'Train duty' was a very popular police occupation. There were few passenger trains running and they were patronised by military customers more than by Iranians. It entailed a 24-hour journey to Ahwaz in southern Iran, 400 miles away and back. This duty fell to my lot in July.

Boarding the train at Teheran station for an 8 a.m. start on July 5th, a Military Police corporal and myself settled down for the long haul through a land of contrasts, a land of hot shimmering deserts, of huge mountain ranges capped with snow, a land occupied and made use of by alien forces.

Iranian trains were slow and the journey across the hot desert to Qum lasted five hours. The only other traffic was American. I remembered our first meeting with an American supply train south of Qum and felt a desire to wave and cheer whenever I saw one. Another five hours of hot desert and the train pulled in to Sultanabad. This dusty little town, its older name was Arak, marked the end of the desert region and the start of the mountain barrier. Sultanabad was green and fertile and though hot and dusty was restful to the eyes.

From here on the railway represented a triumph of engineering. The gradients and tunnels forced a slow pace but there was added time to admire the vistas of mountain scenery that were breathtaking. At 7.00 a.m. we emerged from the last tunnel and left the mountains behind on reaching Andimeshk.

With its back to the soaring peaks, Andi-meshk faced a great flat plain that stretched nearly 200 miles to the Persian Gulf.

Ahwaz lay about 90 miles south across the plain from Andimeshk and was an important centre for the oil industry. We arrived there at eleven in the morning of July 6th and I had already forgotten the warning given by our friends back in Teheran that in Ahwaz – 'it is so hot even the flies die'. Stepping on to the platform was stepping into an oven. The train door handle was too hot to hold. The outdoor temperature was 137 degrees Fahrenheit. A military police motor-cycle combination was there to meet us and the sidecar seat was so hot I jumped up with a yell of pained surprise. The town was deserted, not even a dog stirred. Leaves on the trees lining the streets hung limp and motionless, covered in dust. Apparently in Ahwaz particularly in July, the accepted order was 'on the backs down' until evening when the temperature became tolerable. We drifted along to the premises of the Anglo-Iranian Oil Company and watched an open-air cinema showing of *The Mark of Zorro*.

The train ride to Ahwaz had been a memorable experience and I eagerly antici-pated the return trip the following day for there was nothing in Ahwaz that I would be sorry to leave except the good humour and hospitality of the Military Police unfortunate enough to be stationed there. The return train reached Andimeshk about 11.00 p.m. after leaving Ahwaz five hours earlier and commenced the slow laborious climb into the mountains and its tortuous many-tunnelled journey to the north.

There was a stop at Do-Roud, a mid-mountain halt that I had slept through on the journey south. The light of dawn gave an added mystery and magnificence to the silent eternal mountains as the train laboured along a narrow lofty ledge over-hanging a rapid flowing river.

Protruding from its turbulent current were the rusty bones of a goods train and its engine, like a victim of the wrath of the mountain gods whose peace it had disturbed. Leaving Sultanabad for the long haul to Teheran as the sun reached its zenith I felt the apprehension of the ancient explorers venturing out into the uncharted oceans, to challenge the elements. That vast cauldron of a desert threatened to swallow the unwary traveller. Eventually the dark mass of the Elburz range loomed through the vibrant heat haze and our journey ended 26 hours after leaving Ahwaz. Normal police work I feared was likely to be rather mundane.

Back to street patrol the next day, another free dinner at the Free Hungarian restaurant in the Avenue Lalezar and time to contemplate the strange ways of the East. Our old battalion friends were often met in the streets trying desperately to enjoy their leave. Off duty we would meet them for an evening together. A visit to an Iranian cinema is one way for East and West to meet. I took a friend to see *Elizabeth and Essex* and it was a typical experience. There was an excited swirling mob at the box office. No queue. Only the British form queues. We could only push into the crowd and elbow our way in. The corridors to the auditorium were narrow and we were propelled by the pressure of struggling bodies and reached our seats gasping for breath. The seats were worn threadbare and were rickety with age. The film was interrupted every few minutes and a resumé in Arabic script was screened and we waited as patiently as we were able while those who could read explained it all to those who could not. This gave rise to a lively buzz of conversation often interrupted by unexplainable laughter before the film was resumed. To further complicate the issue the projectionist played the reels in a wrong sequence. Leaving the cinema we had to fight our way through customers coming in for the next performance and we emerged into the street battered but triumphant.

Our last duty with the Military Police was an out-of-bounds house search and it was one to remember. A similar dwelling to the first such house I entered, it stood alone on waste ground. We formed a cordon round the house and courtyard to prevent any escapes over the wall. From outside we could see the second floor balcony with bedroom doors leading off and the upper-most rungs of the ladder giving access from below. Lieutenant Hardy and Sergeant Lawrence opened the door to the courtyard and entered the premises and immediately four scantily clad dusky Armenian girls flitted up the ladder like disturbed butter-flies and fled into the upper floor rooms. As we in the cordon outside waited, the down-stairs search began and two men completely naked who confessed to being British were given two minutes to dress. Meanwhile to our intense interest outside, two British sailors scrambled up the ladder, sprinted along the balcony and entered the room at the far end where a beautiful Persian rug was hanging on the wall. We saw them pull the rug to one side to reveal an alcove in the wall into which they climbed, allowing the rug to hang naturally to complete their concealment. In a few minutes the officer and sergeant scaled the ladder to search the upper floor. They entered the far room closing the door and re-emerged alone and descended the ladder. They re-appeared through the courtyard door with their two victims now fully dressed. They were both

Royal Army Medical Corps officers from the army hospital who surrendered their names and departed sheepishly. By mutual agreement no mention was made of the sailors until our duty was over for the night. When we asked Lieutenant Hardy if he had seen them behind the wall rug he waxed furious, said we should all be court-martialled for not telling him earlier and but for the fact it was our last duty we would have been and he stormed off in apparent high dudgeon. His anger was out of character, a little forced, and we ended the day not quite sure who was fooling who.

The Very Important Person

On August 29th after a farewell dinner the previous evening we left our Redcap friends to rejoin the battalion then encamped near Sultanabad. We had enjoyed our spell of duty in the streets of Teheran, had learned much about the Iranians though little of their language, Farsi. Apart from the conventional Arabic greeting – *Salaam Aleikum* – Peace be with you – we relied in typical British fashion on their command of English which in some cases was superior to our own. I carried memories that would live with me. Memories of the snow on the mountains, of bustling streets and a dead horse, of elderly Polish women forced to live in tents trying so hard to retain their pride and some human dignity, memories too of a wide diversity of human conditions and of an instruction on the Military Police notice board, headed by the words: 'Action to be taken on finding a dead person on the street'.

There was a party of Russian soldiers, some of them girls, on the morning train from Teheran. They were a jolly bunch and as the train commenced its journey towards that hot desert leading to Qum the girls decided to eat. I sat next to one who was opening a tin of Fray Bentos corned beef. She withdrew a wicked-looking knife from her jackboot and proceeded to dig out the contents of the tin which she enjoyed with hunks of bread. She smiled and offered it to all and sundry. For her second course she produced a supply of nuts similar to almonds and a huge pebble to crack them with. The train seats were of plain wooden slats with no upholstery and placing her nuts on the seat she plied her stone nutcracker with gusto. Splintered nut shells were flying all over the compartment and I withdrew amid peals of laughter. We alighted at Sultanabad ten hours from Teheran and rejoined the battalion in the hot arid foothills of the great mountains. We were back, reluctantly.

Though the war fronts were a world away, training was never neglected. It was a major occupation at any time. The Commanding Officer decided the battalion should organise a training course for snipers. Those with good records on the rifle ranges were selected for this training, whether they liked it or not. I liked it. It would be a welcome diversion from routine. Normal battalion life could be dull in those dry remote regions. There were few chances of escape. There was nowhere to go so what could be wrong about a snipers' course?

A sniper is an individualist. He works alone. There were many hours spent on a makeshift rifle range using a telescopic sight. A day on the ranges can be traumatic for those who, through no fault of their own, just cannot master an army rifle. At the end of the day they have a sore shoulder, semi-deafness and a low score. For the others it can be very satisfying, from the moment when the live round slides into the breach and the bolt locks home till the butt marker signals a bull. The sniper trainees enjoyed it.

There were hours of lecturing on the subject. A sniper is principally an observer. We studied enemy uniforms, insignia of rank, enemy guns, vehicles and formations, how to use a message pad, how to judge distance, the use of a compass, the art of camouflage and concealment. The sniper's nest is his sovereign territory. No other person comes near. He chooses it and leaves it on his own initiative. He shoots to kill or he does not shoot at all. He is a supreme loner and his enemy dislikes him intensely. The course aroused great interest and the candidates were duly appointed trained snipers and were left to wonder if and when their qualifications would be tested in earnest.

By the end of October we were packing to move yet again, this time to Andimeshk and an advance party had been there for several days erecting a tented camp on the vast flat plain south of the town. The battalion travelled by train in goods wagons as we had in Iraq and it was rough and did not commence before 11.00 p.m. The mountains greeted my waking and though it was my third excursion along the line with the constantly changing panorama of peaks and valleys with their varying colours, shades and shadows each journey could be the first. The discomforts were amply compensated for though the train needed 15 hours to reach Andimeshk.

The camp had been erected several miles south on the flat and treeless plain and presented a picture of military precision with even the tent pegs in straight lines. As we settled in a rumbling of thunder was heard from the south and the darkening skies and lightning flashes posed an ominous threat. Darkness fell with the impending storm almost upon us and a wind of increasing power was threatening the tents. Making a hurried check on the pegs holding the 180-pounder I shared with seven others, it was agreed this was no time to get into bed. The rain started suddenly and was soon a heavy deluge drumming on the canvas and the wind achieved a frightful velocity. The three tent poles were whipping violently so two men clung to each in an attempt to prevent breakage while the thunder crashed and roared overhead. There were shouts and cries around the camp in the inky darkness and we knew disaster had struck. The wind velocity increased beyond anything we had ever experienced and the tent bucked and billowed like an ungainly bird trying to take to its wings. Suddenly it collapsed and the screaming wind and sheeting rain swept over us and all our possessions. Personal belongings, clothing, anything we did not actually lie on top of was snatched away as by an unseen hand and disappeared for ever.

Having wreaked havoc, the rain stopped abruptly, the wind dropped and the storm rumbled and flashed its way north leaving us in cold and miserable confusion waiting for a merciful dawn. The new day revealed utter chaos. Not a single tent was left standing. A large marquee housing our arms and ammunition had been smashed and flattened, exposing its contents to the elements. News soon spread of tragedy. In an adjacent camp, now in a similar condition, was an artillery battery that travelled and trained with the Royal Sussex. One of their officers used a folding metal bedstead in his tent, which became airborne when his tent collapsed and it struck the battalion adjutant causing a severe injury from which he died. There were broken arms and sprains and bruises and a considerable loss of clothing. Some who had unwisely undressed for bed were left with very little.

Andimeshk provided us with an insight to the organisation behind the American supply of war material to Russia. Components of heavy lorries built by the General Motors Corporation were shipped to the Iranian port of Khorramshahr in huge wooden crates and distributed to various assembly camps set up in the area, one of which was situated in Andimeshk. After assembly they were loaded with war material of every description. Much Iranian labour was employed in the camps and some Iranians actually drove the assembled and loaded vehicles through the mountains and deserts to the Russian border. Road check points were manned by Military

Police and the Royal Sussex men to prevent pilfering but nevertheless large amounts of material were lost. If the load was of a saleable nature, such as food, the driver was tempted to sell it on his way north and then drive the truck into a lonely mountain hide-out and sell the tyres, batteries and anything else he found a market for and disappear rich beyond his wildest dreams. The Special Investigation Branch of the Military Police found many an abandoned shell but later the drivers were American and eventually Russians were roaring through amid swirling dust.

The Americans at Andimeshk allowed us to take possession of many dismantled crates and we worked late and long in the construction of a mess hall for our use. We were proud of the finished building in spite of the stencilled wording 'General Motors' and 'This Side Up' which adorned it. Perhaps it was fortunate the storm that greeted our arrival never repeated itself.

The railway was also revealing its wartime history. Prior to the coming of the Americans many old English railway engines had been converted to oil-burning and conscripted for use in Iran. They were now to be seen shunted into sidings and left to end their days in idle rusty retirement. They looked rather sad. Old servants of the G.W.R. and the L.M.S. lost and dying in an alien goods yard. They had been superseded by the giant American locomotives such as greeted us so warmly on the lonely desert road to Qum. These too, were being replaced by the diesel engines of more modern times. Powerful and functionally ugly, they lacked the romantic aura of the giant steamers but were impressive evidence of the American flair for engineering and organisation. The old steam engines were still working, stubbornly refusing to die, and in the dead of night their low moaning whistle issuing from the dark brooding mountains sounded like the cry of a lost soul.

The Kharun river rushed from the mountains near Andimeshk where it had carved a deep channel for itself as it made its way south to the Shatt El Arab. On the eastern bank on high ground overlooking the river stood the little town of Dizful. A bridge spanned the high banks giving access to Dizful but not for us for it had been ruled strictly out of bounds. Across the river the high steep bank was honeycombed with caves that were inhabited. The town itself was up to three storeys high, mainly of mud brick construction and intersected by narrow alleys. There was so much disease and blindness in the area no one desired to challenge the out-of-bounds ruling. Extensive graveyards could be seen on the town outskirts and when the wind blew from the east the poverty of Dizful became apparent. Some cave dwellers lived on the Andimeshk side of the river. Thick pungent smoke emerged from the cave entrances when cow-dung fires were burning and old women could often be seen looming through the smoke and dressed in their traditional long black attire with dark wrinkled faces they bore a witch-like aspect.

Of all the afflictions of poverty to be seen in Iran, blindness was the most prevalent and the most distressing to observe. With an area the size of Central Europe and poor communications, medical services were practically non-existent and though we had seen heart-breaking deprivation and desti-tution in Egypt, the sufferings of the Iranian masses scattered in small communities in remote places was even more desperate. Food shortages were endemic and Iran relied heavily on imported grain. There had been civil disturbances in Teheran in 1941 because of a desperate wheat shortage, where stocks were at one time down to one day's needs. A range of grain silos stood by the railway sidings in Teheran emphasising the importance of the rail link with the Gulf ports.

The railway, so vital to Iran's domestic needs, and also to the Allies, was built by foreign engineers before the war. There had been great loss of life among Iranian workers from disease in the construction gangs and a cartoon often displayed in Teheran depicted a length of track with skeletons lying in the place of sleepers in support of a claim that there was one death for every sleeper laid. Most of the rolling stock that was not American was of German manufacture and the passenger coaches bore the nameplate of Krupps of Essen. The stations were German built and the main hall of Teheran station carried a swastika design in the ceiling plaster and a statue of the reigning Shah's father, Riza Pahlevi, stood facing the streets on horseback giving a Nazi salute.

Having restored our shattered camp to some sort of order, we settled down to the prospect of activity to which the area lent itself – mountain training. Our training was often held in conjunction with the Royal Artillery battery whose neighbouring camp suffered the same fate in the storm that greeted our arrival. There was a well-remembered occasion when during an exercise using live ammunition they dropped a shell short and wounded one of our number. From that day forth they were the 'Chinese Gunners'.

The end of November saw a break in training for myself and five others. We were informed that a Very Important Person was coming to Iran and we were a chosen escort party. We were to go to Khorramshahr, the main Gulf port and await his coming and act as escorts on the train journey to Teheran. The identity of the V.I.P. was denied us. Leaving the camp by truck at the unearthly hour of 2.15 a.m. to catch a train at Andimeshk on November 24th we learned there was no train so the journey was completed by road. This entailed driving 80 miles to Ahwaz and another 100 miles to Khorramshahr. The plain was absolutely flat the whole way and the road from Ahwaz had just one slight bend in its entire length. The mystery surrounding this affair intrigued us. Great emphasis had been laid on personal appearances. We had all been warned to 'smarten up a bit' and 180 miles of dusty road travel did not help. On arrival we were billeted in an empty warehouse and set about the task of removing the stains of travel with some traditional spit and polish. Our stay in waiting lasted six days.

At evening time we were allowed out to visit a services' club, an American camp or to cross the Shatt El Arab to the Royal Navy base to enjoy a good meal or a cinema show but during the day we could only wait and wonder who needed an escort and when. We never saw the streets of Khorramshahr in daylight. There were long debates and discussions about the possible identity of the mysterious Very Important Person and various suggestions were bandied about. It would hardly be a general for generals did not rank such an escort. The King was even mentioned but why would the King come to Iran? Winston Churchill was another suggestion, not considered very likely to be using the Iranian railway. He was at that time attending a conference in Cairo with President Roosevelt and Chiang Kai-Shek. There was no way we could solve the riddle, so we resigned ourselves to wait till the great man arrived at Khorramshahr. Which he never did.

On the morning of December 3rd we were informed quite bluntly that the whole thing was off and it was back to the battalion forthwith. Our disappointment was profound. To escort whoever it might have been 600 miles across the deserts and through those fabulous mountains was an experience we hated to miss. Our sense of loss and frustration was increased when the secret was revealed. Churchill had arrived in Teheran by plane from Cairo for a conference with Stalin and Roosevelt. The train had been a stand-by arrangement in case bad weather made a flight over the mountains inadvisable. However, we had enjoyed six days holiday and arrived back at Andimeshk with some of the spit and polish still visible.

Returning to battalion service after a special detachment was always a chastening experience. There was still a war to be won and a state of readiness for it to be preserved. For that reason, high in the mountains beyond Andimeshk a mountain warfare camp had been established and my company were ready to move there when I arrived back from Khorramshahr.

Another early reveille and we drove into the mountains along an exciting road that wound its way into another world. Leaving the road to negotiate a rough track, we found the camp surrounded by massive peaks, ranges, crags and valleys set in fantastic shapes and forms as if the earth's crust had been slashed by a gigantic cosmic knife. Nearby a crystal-clear stream had formed a narrow pool between high rocks. This was the camp swimming pool. It was sheltered and deep and was clear melted snow. We spent happy hours in its chilly depths but it was mountain training we came for and it was mountain training we endured. It was strenuous to a degree. With lungs almost bursting and legs that refused to respond to our wills, we envied the nimble gazelle we sometimes encountered as they floated over the rocks and boulders with fairy-like grace and incredible speed. Our exertions were constantly rewarded by the magnificent vistas that awaited us around every corner.

The region was also occupied by a

nomadic tribe who were encamped within a mile of us. An Iranian interpreter accompanied us during our sojourn in the mountains to prevent any unfortunate clash with them during training exercises. He explained the tribe paid no allegiance to the Shah's Government, had no knowledge of current affairs, had never heard of Hitler, Stalin or Churchill but had a vague idea we were there to protect Teheran. They shepherded a flock of sheep and goats and a few bony cattle that grazed the valleys nearby while the grazing lasted. Near their camp was a crudely cultivated patch sown with wheat and a little burial ground with each grave marked by a lump of rock. The elderly and the very young stayed near the camp with a motley collection of chicken and dogs while the able menfolk and children tended the flock. They also possessed some hardy ponies ridden bareback by the young men with great agility. As the flock moved through the valleys an occasional animal would lag behind and take time off to give birth and then hasten to rejoin the flock. The tribe was self-sufficient. Their animals provided meat, milk, fur, skins and transport and when the grazing had been exhausted the time had come to find pastures new, to return later when the grass had renewed itself and the wheat could be harvested. Primitive, pastoral and with a degree of

107

freedom many could envy.

The young men of the tribe took a great interest in our swimming activities and would ride their ponies across the intervening boulder-strewn expanse at a reckless speed and watch us very earnestly. They seemed to regard swimming as peculiar behaviour past their understanding.

At the end of the second week it rained and if it rains in Iran it rains hard and we were in yet another muddy camp. We never saw it dry again but the training programme was completed in the rain or not in the rain, and it rained for most of four days.

December 22nd was chosen as the day of our return to the battalion at Andimeshk. The same day was also chosen as moving day by our nomadic neighbours. Both parties chose the same track and the same time of day and the outcome was bizarre. The sheep and goats went ahead of the tribal column followed by the cows with, incredibly, the chicken sitting on their backs, necks and between their horns. Infant lambs and kids were hung over the cows' backs in string nets. Likewise an infant child. The elderly sat on elderly ponies and the young men and boys rode other ponies. Other able-bodied members of the strange and picturesque procession were on foot.

The two parties became merged into one column of sheep and trucks, cows and jeeps and goats and motor cycles and moved at a slow walking pace. It was a unique blending of two strange cultures.

Arriving back at the camp we found the great plain had acquired a fresh coat of green grass and the camp itself a coat of thick mud. We anticipated a thoroughly miserable Christmas but in fact the Christmas day was warm and sunny and we enjoyed a first-class Christmas dinner of turkey 'and all the trimmings' in our USA, GENERAL MOTORS, THIS SIDE UP mess room. In deference to tradition, the officers waited at table and our company commander dressed up as Santa Claus.

Yankee

Meanwhile in Teheran the Military Police had divested themselves of responsibility for the security of the transit camp near the hospital. It had been handed over to Regimental Police from the Royal Sussex who were due to be relieved by a party from our battalion. I considered myself to be very fortunate to be one of those selected. I had not expected to see Teheran again or to escape yet again the routine of battalion life. Six of us plus a sergeant boarded a train at

Andimeshk late at night and slept our way through the mountains to Sultanabad and I awoke to face yet another excursion across the yawning void, the hot dusty expanse of sun, sand and salt to Teheran via Qum.

My return to Teheran was on January 11th 1944. The contrast to my arrival on May Day, the previous year epitomised the nature and climate of Iran. The contrast of extremes. Desert and mountains, the rich and the destitute, the ancient and the modern, farming land and salt lakes, sweltering heat and snow and all in a day's travel. The Elburz mountains were completely enveloped in a thick white shroud and the cone of Demavend was a thick frozen pointer to the heavens. The streets were sprinkled with snow and an icy wind chilled us as we emerged from the railway station. This was Teheran with a difference and we were glad to reach our destination – 109 Transit Camp.

The guard-room building included an armoury and several lock-up cells and a smoky coke stove for heating. The take-over procedure included signing for an inventory of goods and chattels and included in the list was one prisoner. No ordinary prisoner this. He was tall, young and handsome and he was American. Clad in a smart American uniform he sported three French medal ribbons. He welcomed us with a cheer and humour that belied his station. His farewells to his departing gaolers were prolonged and heartfelt. His bed was in a cell but he enjoyed the freedom of the camp and when we had arranged our sleeping accommodation and sorted our kit, in that order, we sat around the stove and fired questions at him.

Why? we demanded, was an American being held in custody by the British with an American camp only two miles distant. He had been introduced to us as 'Yankee'. According to the inventory his name was Ian MacNeil but as he was content with 'Yankee' the name 'stuck'. He explained to us that he was a deserter from the Free French Air Force and had no connection with the American forces. The United States only maintained Railroad Operating Companies in Teheran. The British maintained garrison troops so he was our prisoner and he was obviously very happy with the arrangement. He was an engaging character. A cultured good-mannered young man and full of fun despite his bizarre circumstances. He was obsessed with the coke stove which he stoked up frequently and fed with anything combustible he could lay his hands on. In the warmth of its smoky glow he unfolded his life's history. Or some of it. What he told us was greeted with scepticism, for we all felt he was a 'line-shooter'. True or false, it was a good story.

His mother was American. His father a Scot. He was born in Germany near Dusseldorf. His childhood years were spent in Paris. He spoke French with an easy fluency. As a youth he lived in London and travelled extensively around the United Kingdom. His knowledge of our homeland was astonishing. In the United States when war was declared he went to France, joined their Air Force and flew fighter planes. After the French capitulation he joined the Free French in Africa and flew in the desert campaigns. After the Alamein victory he deserted for reasons he would not divulge. Iran had many foreign troops in its streets but the French were absent so Yankee hitched a lift by plane to Teheran in true American fashion and presented himself to the military attaché at the United States Embassy who, not knowing what else to do with an American deserter from the Free French, handed him over to the British, to await a French escort.

He regarded his future with easy confidence. Our assurances that he would be court-martialled and probably shot at dawn did not dismay him. According to Yankee the French could not court-martial an American citizen. This point was argued in true barrack-room lawyer style. Most of Yankee's claims provoked argument which never failed to delight him. His medals he averred consisted of the *Croix de Guerre* and two wound medals. Hoots of derision greeted his claim to the honours and his affirmation that he was a personal friend of General Eisenhower was laughed out of court. However his claims could not be disproved. He took a roguish delight in poking fun at anything British and on occasions the air was warm in spite of his attentions to the coke stove.

Periodically he received a cheque by post from his grandmother in California. This necessitated an escorted trip into a bank in Teheran to change it into Iranian rials, followed by a shopping spree. On one occasion he treated himself to a huge sheepskin coat that reached from his ears to his ankles giving him a weird shaggy appearance evoking much good-natured derision which he enjoyed immensely.

His only complaint about the conditions of his custody was the absence of a decent bath. On one memorable occasion I escorted him into Teheran for a visit to the public baths. At the pay desk he asked me how I proposed to escort him while he bathed. I assured him I would be waiting for him but he suggested I must need a bath as urgently as he so why not join him and we could scrub each other's back? I yielded at once and we entered a room with a large sunken bath with an abundance of hot water. He tossed his American uniform with its three French medal ribbons into one corner to be joined by mine with its solitary Africa Star ribbon and our respective military relationships went with them. Yankee sang in the bath, with more gusto than harmony, and after a mutual scrub-down we eventually emerged as escort and prisoner clean and glowing.

Yankee resided with us, as our prisoner, quite happily for several weeks. He slept soundly and rose with reluctance. He was usually late for breakfast. His parents were never mentioned or any friends, with the possible exception of General Eisenhower, and his only mail was the occasional cheque from his grandmother. How much of his story was true we never knew. The up-heavals and contortions of war produce many stories stranger than fiction, many people drift, rootless, on the stormy seas of fortune before being cast ashore on an alien beach. There was a basic sadness about Yankee that his bonhomie failed to conceal. He had lost control of his life.

A senior French officer arrived in 109 Transit Camp one day. We all knew his mission. Yankee shrugged his shoulders and commenced packing. His sheepskin coat was quite a problem. The next morning the Frenchman presented himself at the guardroom to collect his prisoner. He was stern and quite immaculate. Military correct in every way. In British army parlance, he was 'regimental as a button-stick'. The farewells began in earnest and the rigid Frenchman was obviously not in sympathy with our unique prisoner-gaoler relationships. It was a sad moment for us all for we were losing a friend rather than a prisoner. The sergeant agreed to see him off at the airport. Yankee's good cheer never left him and as the truck moved out of the camp he waved like a small boy going on holiday. The plane soared into the Iranian sky and set course for Damascus and Yankee vanished from our lives. Someone remarked that he would not be up in time to be shot at dawn. Whatever was to happen, we hoped the French would be lenient for if he had a love in his life, it was for France.

The Regimental Police duty at the camp went on for five months. It was an easy and relatively comfortable spell of duty. In common with many of my fellows, I experienced moments of unease about the duration of our role in Iran. We were making so little effort in the war itself we sometimes felt 'spare'. Our presence may have been necessary but it seemed so indirect and ineffectual. Some were happy to be well away from the war fronts. Others were genuinely interested in their surroundings and welcomed the opportunity to see 'how the other half lived' and were content to be where they were sent which was perhaps the most practical attitude. Iran was a military backwater, a whirlpool just off the main-stream of war and all who were caught in it floated round in unending circles. However for those with seeing eyes there was little cause for boredom.

We were glad to feel the approach of summer for Teheran in the snow was a cheerless place. Destitutes on the streets suffered a greater misery that was painful to behold. Snow and high winds swirled mercilessly around the street corners and one night in the camp an army hut lost its entire roof in one piece leaving the Sikh officer sleeping therein covered in rubble. It was my pleasure occasionally to meet a familiar figure among the Military Police on duty in the streets of Teheran. Having enjoyed a unique insight to their life, I regarded them in a more sympathetic light than many of my colleagues. There came an episode concerning the Redcaps that provided a further insight to their duties and attendant problems. Three of us from the transit camp police were sent to the railway goods yard with a lorry to collect a consignment of Iranian bank notes for delivery to a bank in the city centre. Standing alone in a siding were two enclosed rail wagons with two Indian soldiers and two military policemen. One wagon had been used for accommodation and the other contained the precious cargo.

The notes were packed in large crates and there were so many our lorry was hardly large enough and the load required ropes. The consignment had been produced in England and shipped to Basra where the Military Police took charge of them in a marshalling yard used by the American forces. The Redcaps were under strict orders not to divulge the nature of the load to anyone under any circumstances.

The American sergeant in charge of the yard asked for details of the goods before he would couple it to a Teheran-bound train. He was far from pleased when his request was refused. He replied in very direct terms that until such time they deigned to supply him with the requested details the wagons remained where they stood. So a small scale private Anglo-American war broke out. Neither side would yield to the other on principle. The hapless Redcaps and their two Indian soldiers sat out the stalemate for ten days, before the Americans finally yielded and hitched them to a goods train.

They helped us load the crates with great relief having cared for them for two weeks. Their duty was done and ours began. Armed with rifles we climbed on top of the load and drove through the streets of

Teheran feeling like Wild West characters riding 'shotgun'. It would have been interesting to have known the value of the goods we were sitting on. A lorry load of paper money – the mind boggled.

Arriving at the bank, we drove to the rear of the building where I was surprised to see large immaculate lawns and rose beds. A rare sight in Iran – a lovely peaceful garden. Ambling across the grass was an elegant domestic cat. A Persian cat by residential qualifications if not by breed and the only cat I ever saw in Iran. We unloaded the crates on the gravel drive or on the grass and waited for a director of the bank to open the vaults so we could complete our delivery. When he arrived he explained in good English it needed directors with different keys to open the vaults. We had hoped to see the bank vaults, but the director happily signed for the consignment and we bade him farewell. It was perhaps fortunate the two Military Policemen who had devoted two weeks at great personal discomfort to safeguard the crates did not see them lying unguarded all over the garden.

The Deep Blue Sea

On the 23rd May my old battalion, in its entirety, moved into 109 Transit Camp and I knew the days of my police duty were nearly over. They were not staying long. I rejoined them a week later and the next day we set out on a journey that was to take us 1,400 miles to the shores of the Mediterranean Sea. A long ride, a rough ride, but to pastures new. Our destination was the little country of Lebanon. Rumour had it the purpose was for mountain training prior to a possible move to Italy. Rumours were greeted with scepticism but rumour was all we had. Whatever the purpose, we were on the move and I welcomed it and was eager to see the Mediterranean once more. The nearest sea to Teheran, excluding the Caspian, was the Gulf and that was 600 miles away. Not many of Teheran's masses ever saw the sea in their lifetime.

The convoy moved off through the suburbs and I made my silent farewells. My feelings were mixed. Glad to be going, yet sad. Streets that on my arrival were foreign, with the excitement of the unknown, the strangeness of another planet, now had the appeal of familiarity. The railway station slipped behind us, the goods yards, the grain silos and Teheran was in my past. The final view was the first view. The Elburz mountains with the rising snowline revealing the lower slopes.

First stop was to be Qum after another trek across the sweltering miles, with the blinding salt lakes. Of all desert journeys I had memories of there was none worse than those 90 miles between Teheran and Qum. Low lying and hemmed in by mountains, it shimmered with heat. On a train the heat was inescapable but the ride was otherwise comfortable though I always had mental visions of the train running out of fuel halfway across and stranding us in jeopardy like an aircraft with failing engines over the Atlantic. In the back end of an Army truck there was little comfort and dust as fine as flour soon covered all and everything. Temperatures were riding high on May 31st and the column raised a huge billowing cloud miles long.

The traveller from Teheran looks for the great golden dome of the Qum mosque. From miles away it beckons the weary and the dusty and the Islamic faithful. This stage of our migration lasted five horrible hours. We stopped in the town while a suitable site for the night was chosen. A passenger train was in the station and a number of travellers moved into the crowded street. Among them, like a vision, was a tall young woman smartly clad in Western style with long black hair and a proud and serene countenance. She was obviously a lady of culture and attainment for two Kurdish porters followed her carrying her luggage. One was burdened with a trunk and several suitcases and the other carried a piano on his back, a little short-lived scene that for me epitomised the incongruities of the Middle East.

The second day of travel was as familiar as the first. 100 miles to Sultanabad. Hot, dusty and infinitely wearying in an army truck, but the practical traveller, like a true nomad, lives by the hope of better things beyond the horizon. Moving on early next morning, the road led us through Malayer where we spent a night on our way to Teheran just over a year previously. The country became gradually green and pro-ductive and pleasant to behold as we wheeled our way westward towards Ker-manshah. It was refreshing to see people working in the little fields surrounded by the fruits of their labours, where man's affinity with the soil finds a natural expression. They bore an air of contentment not found in the city dwellers. Passing the familiar site of the former Royal Sussex camp we had pre-viously left deep in mud, we threaded our way into the mountains and spent the night in and around the same little hut with the walled courtyard amid the lofty silent peaks that our Teheran party had rested in.

Tomorrow would be the day for saying goodbye to Iran. Would it be for ever? Or would we return some day? One of the attractions of wartime travel is the unpredictability. Some 'office wallah' moves a pin on a map and many people's lives are changed. The normal early start and I waited for the thrill of the descent of the Pai-tak Pass into Iraq. It did not disappoint. The views were tremendous. The great flat plain of Iraq was laid out like an aerial photograph and the road twisted down to it with each corner presenting a new hair-raising hazard. As we descended so the temperature rose and on entering Iraq and crossing the plain to Khanaqin we sweltered in 110 degrees Fahrenheit.

Next stop towards the distant sea was Baghdad. From a 5.00 a.m. start we completed the 110 miles to the capital by midday. There was a large swimming pool in the Baghdad transit camp and we were soon in it to remove the strains of long travel and prepare for more. We took the next day off and visited the old city once again. It was very hot and the swimming pool was the main attraction.

With machines and men rested and refreshed we bade farewell to Baghdad at

6.00 a.m. Farewells, but would we meet again? The fortunes of war would decide. Passing through the fertile fringes of the city, we crossed the Euphrates and motored on to the flat and lonely wastelands. The road was good by Middle East standards and we all remembered how long it was. Two days were spent reaching Rutbah. The oppressive temperature caused the most discomfort. The column of vehicles was spaced out over several miles and looking forward the horizon appeared distorted by the heat haze and the leading trucks appeared to float in the air and lose their outline and acquire shimmering reflections of peculiar vibrant forms or appeared to be driving through a shining lake. We were seeing mirages and, like the end of a rainbow, they were tantalising and elusive. A day's journey from Rutbah, alongside the pipeline and the long thin thread of telephone wire, we reached H.4, the lonesome pumping station. We stopped, rested and refuelled and arrived in Jordanian territory. The next day we passed through the black landscape of volcanic rock and reached the flat arid region of Mafraq. From here we moved into unfamiliar country where the land was flat, relatively fertile and cultivated. We were in Syria and heading for Damascus, 100 miles from Mafraq.

Our stay outside Damascus was too brief

for us to visit the city. We were on the move by 7.00 a.m. The road led us away through a long and strikingly beautiful gorge that opened into an expanse of mountainous countryside clothed in greenery and cultivated to as high an altitude as humanly possible. Gone were the hot deserts and barren peaks and huge distances between habitations. We were in a land of pastoral freshness of villages and other wheeled traffic, where the mountain tops were dressed in dark green conifers. A long hill climb lifted us to lofty heights as we approached Beirut and eyes were strained to catch the first glimpse of the sea. A narrow gauge 'rack' railway scaled the heights of the region with a central toothed rail that engaged with a cogwheel under the engine to assist its climb.

As we approached the suburbs of Beirut from the inland heights the longed-for vision was seen. There was no colour in the world like it. The blue Mediterranean Sea. Somehow it made England's shores seem tantalisingly within reach. If only we could sail across its glittering surface! If only! Beirut was the most modern city we had seen since leaving Egypt. Blocks of flats, modern streets. Trams even. The main central thoroughfare lined with palm trees was quite beautiful and the lovely sea front with its large hotels and air of commercial prosperity was a different world. One aspect of Beirut made itself apparent very soon. We were unprepared for the high humidity of the Mediterranean shores. Coming from high temperatures far inland, we found ourselves perspiring profusely with the thermometer 20 degrees lower.

The convoy followed the coastal road northward through a gorgeous panorama of scenery with deep blue water on one side, high conifer-clad hills on the other and an air of good living over all. We reached the village of Chekka and encamped on the seashore. We had left Teheran on May 31st. It was now June 13th and it was officially announced we were staying for a week and during that time the least possible work would be done. We were on our holidays.

The sea was clear, clean and warm. We revelled in it and basked in the sunshine. All the necessary routine work was shared. The cookhouse chores were distributed among the many and soon done. Our rations were augmented by bartering corned beef for eggs and fruit from the residents of Chekka. This was strictly unofficial for it was a flagrant violation of King's Rules and Regulations, but the locals would swap almost anything for corned beef. We were able to visit Tripoli farther along the coast, with truck transport provided. A pretty town, Tripoli, in a beautiful setting with a Crusaders' castle on high ground nearby.

All happy holidays come to an end and on June 19th we moved to a new campsite just inland from Tripoli in an olive grove near the village of Zhagorta. Training was to start in earnest with no more delay. It was a rare pleasure to camp on grass under trees. In the dusk of evening fireflies weaved dancing patterns of light in the warm air and the hum of insects was a reminder of the utter silence and desolation of the deserts we had left behind us.

Training was exhausting in the green mountains of Lebanon partly because of the humidity. We perspired and thirsted greatly but the local water was like cool wine. Some of the villages were set in dramatically beautiful surroundings. Perhaps the most striking was little Dumah. As we approached from high ground that surrounded the valley on three sides where Dumah was hiding from the world, we suddenly were looking down on the rooftops far far below. The view was breathtaking. We approached from above down a narrow tortuous road that snaked its way down and down into a valley rich in grass flowers and cultivation fed and watered by a shallow river. The little houses faced neat well-tended gardens and the villagers watched us pass in calm interest. Crossing the river, we climbed slowly out of the secluded little paradise by a road that clung perilously to a narrow ledge on the brink of a frightful precipice.

The verdant hills and valleys were enriched by nature's aromas from grasses and wild flowers and the refreshing tang of pine. Our eyes, our ears and our noses were reminding us of the natural physical delights of this world that are absent in the great deserts. Not an inch of soil that could be utilised to produce food or fruit was left untilled. The hills were carved into terraces up to dizzy heights and olives were the most prominent crop. Olive groves were to be found in some almost inaccessible places.

Training came to an abrupt halt when a sudden fever swept through the camp. It was extremely unpleasant, producing high temperatures and weakness and so many were afflicted at the same time the life of the battalion was seriously disrupted. Who cares for the sick when the medical staff are ill? Who feeds the hungry when the catering staff are flat on their backs? Who leads the rank and file when the officers can barely stand up? The fever ran only for a few days and once begun recovery was rapid and our strenuous programme was soon resumed.

Our old friends, the Chinese Gunners, were still with us and we trusted them with live ammunition on occasions and with the sea within easy access our aching limbs were relieved by the most beautiful swimming conditions imaginable. We all fell in love with Lebanon, this jewel of the Mediterranean shore. A day's leave in Beirut was another pleasure that came our way and it was all too good to last. Rumours were being transmitted to receptive ears. We were not bound for Italy after all. Burma maybe. One thing was certain. We were not likely to be going home. The same training continued but we were unsure whether it was officially mountain or jungle warfare we were preparing for. There was no noticeable difference. In mid-August our next move was revealed to us. It surprised us all. We were not going to Italy or Burma, or not yet. We were going back to Teheran. The little man in his office had moved the pin back.

The United Nations

The news was received with some dismay and bewilderment. There were some who wearied of deserts and barren mountains and long rough journeys. It was generally realised there had been no likelihood of a prolonged stay on the Mediterranean shore but there had existed hopes of leaving the Middle East for Europe. The question of why we had travelled 1,400 miles from Teheran only to trek the whole way back within 12 weeks was difficult to answer. There were various explanations offered for debate, none very logical so it was light-heartedly agreed it was a ruse 'to impress the natives' and 'ours was not to reason why'.

If our ultimate destination was to be Burma at least we were moving in the right direction and on August 19th we left Zhagorta camp at 5.00 a.m. and took a long sad look at the deep blue sea as we motored along the coastal road to Beirut. Driving through the city centre and climbing to the heights behind the metropolis, we bade farewell to Lebanon regretfully with a sound conviction we would never see it again. It had given our sensory organs a treat to remember and I felt the whole excursion had been worthwhile just to let me see the village of Dumah.

The great gorge that funnelled us into Damascus was as lovely as I remembered it but we were again unable to explore the city. Another day's travel and we were back to Mafraq and faced the long straight road to H.4, Rutbah and Baghdad. At one point the flickering blue light of a welding operation on the pipeline could be seen beyond the distant horizon where the road's perspective reduced it to a point. Hours later we passed the working party and near the end of our day we looked back and saw the same scene in reverse. As before, we stayed a whole day on Lancer Camp, the transit camp in Baghdad, and next day set forth for Khanaqin, then across the hot plain, up the Pai-tak Pass, through Kermanshah, Malayer and Sultanabad. Then, for me, the seventh time, across the cauldron of a desert to Qum and Teheran where we arrived on September 1st. We settled into a camp on the wasteland north of the city just a stone's throw from 109 Transit Camp. Having spent more time in Teheran than most of my colleagues, I felt a twinge of the embarrassment of a guest who, having made a fond and final farewell, arrives back on his host's doorstep almost immediately.

The battalion was soon back in training with the emphasis on shooting. A rifle range was built a few miles away and each company spent a whole week trying to achieve a four-inch group at 100 yards and other such exercises. It was easy for the snipers.

Back from the rifle ranges I awaited the next diversion. There was not long to wait. 'You, you, you and you.' My military superiors were at it again.

'Get yourself smartened up, you are going to the fair.'

Anything for a change but this was to be no ordinary fair. Not a 'Hey, Nonny No' type British fair, but a United Nations' Fair, no less. In Kazvin. I had never heard of Kazvin but soon discovered its whereabouts. 90 miles north west of Teheran. Red Army country. The United Nations we had all heard of and wished it well.

October 6th, 8.00 a.m. and our little party were truck-borne and on the way to lend support to the U.N. There was a snag or two in it for us. The fair was to open at 6.00 p.m. on the morrow. Before going to the fair we were required to erect it, or at least the British section. The other snag was only 20 miles of the 90 was good road. The other 70 was very rough and dusty. The sort of road to which we had become accustomed but we had dutifully smartened ourselves up. Dust soon covered us like a grey shroud. The Elburz mountains were looming nearer as we journeyed but the road was so bad and the dust cloud so thick the view was not appreciated.

We were accommodated at an American camp on the outskirts of Kazvin. They greeted us after over 5 hours of punishing travel and fed us well. The afternoon was spent spitting out the dust and restoring our respectability. The camp was a 'stop-over' for Americans driving supply trucks to Russia. They were getting on with the war while we were off to the fair.

There was a large open square in the centre of Kazvin with a sunken area in the centre a few steps below street level. This was the site chosen for the fair and we reported the next morning to commence work. The British Council was the body responsible for the British section. It consisted mainly of stands displaying literature extolling the British Way of Life. There were books and pamphlets on the British Parliamentary System, British History, The Industrial Revolution and British Agriculture. The Council was very thorough and we worked dutifully hard and all was ready and suitably be-flagged by the appointed opening hour.

The town streets swarmed with Russian soldiers nearly all carrying sub-machine guns. They were neither hostile nor friendly. Just indifferent. The language barrier was complete. This was their territory and we were being tolerated. The United States' section of the fair was typically American, a jazz band. The Indian section also provided a band and the host nation, Iran, also had a musical representation.

The arena was soon overcrowded. The British section was protected by two armed Indian guards to prevent too much of the British Way of Life being purloined. Darkness fell, the fairy lights draped around the fair lent a festive air and spirits rose. All three bands played at the same time producing a unique United Nations' sound. Bedlam. Drinks flowed unchecked. Everyone was toasting everyone else. The Russians continued patrolling the streets while everyone except the Indians drank recklessly. The British contingent consumed more liquor than they should have and the American jazz band was soon in disarray.

The jolly party continued into the night but by 1.00 a.m. it was dying slowly from lack of support. The British squad was in no condition to continue the revelry and the American jazz pianist lay slumped across the keyboard! We returned to our United States' hosts about 1.30 a.m. and they were serving hot coffee. It was undoubtedly the best cup of coffee ever made. They were perfect hosts but we were far from perfect guests. Our going to bed was a long and noisy process and raised angry protests from American drivers trying to sleep after a long day on the road and another to follow.

Came the dawn and some very British hangovers. The return journey was a ghastly prospect in our condition. We were not ready to leave before noon, and our American hosts must have been delighted to see us go. We all sat silently in the bouncing dust-shrouded vehicle trying to keep body and soul together for 90 miles. The awful journey was over by 5.00 p.m. and the British delegation to the United Nations' Assembly withdrew from public gaze to complete their recovery. It would probably be true to say the various nationals present at the Kazvin fair were united in one respect. They would all have preferred to be home. A message of thanks was duly received from the British Council for our contribution to the event but we secretly hoped if it was to be an annual occurrence we would be thousands of miles away next year. Preferably to the westward. The most vivid memory was the return journey, the vigours of which outweighed all the fun of the fair.

Before October was out there was another you, you and you session that embroiled me once more. This was a rush job. Grab haversack rations from the cookhouse and be ready. In Iran there were a number of civilian detainees. Any persons suspected of plotting against the Allied cause were arrested and confined in a detention camp in Sultanabad. Three of these detainees had been handed over some time previously to the Russians and they were now being returned to British care. Our brief was to collect them at Teheran airport and return them to Sultanabad. I wilted at the prospect of crossing that punishing desert yet again – and back. It was not like the Egyptian desert or any other desert of my acquaintance. It was an ordeal 190 miles long and only Qum to relieve the weary nomad.

With two trucks, a lieutenant and a sergeant and two escorts per vehicle we drove to the airport and waited at the end of a runway. A Russian lorry appeared and the three detainees were transferred after brief formalities. Two were allocated to one vehicle and the other, a heavily-robed and bearded priest, together with myself and a colleague, climbed aboard the remaining vehicle. With his luggage and voluminous attire, there was little room to spare. The little convoy returned to camp to allow our prisoners and ourselves some sustenance for the impending trek through the dust.

Our starting time was 2.15 p.m. and we all knew it would be late at night before we reached Sultanabad. Our priest remained silent throughout the journey. By pulling the canvas flaps together at the rear we endeavoured to keep out some of the dust, but he was soon covered from head to foot and his two escorts were being slowly smothered as they sat near the tailboard. With the coming of darkness we sat in complete gloom and silence and lived with our own thoughts. I felt sympathy for our prisoner who maintained an air of dignity in his rather humiliating situation and I wondered how the real war was being pursued while we three sat enveloped in darkness in a rocking vehicle bouncing in mid-desert.

Suddenly our truck left the road with a sickening lurch sideways and stopped. With some alarm I jumped out, fearing a breakdown. Both trucks had left the road and with good reason. A huge convoy of American lorries driven by Russian soldiers was approaching at high speed. Their glaring headlights' beams were reflected by a thick cloud of swirling dust. They roared past us in a floodlit fog miles long. Leaving the road had prevented us being smashed to pieces. It was an opportunity to eat our sandwiches which we shared with our charges, who indicated their gratitude, and we watched the weird and noisy illuminated spectacle as it hurtled by. It was a novel behind-the-scenes view of the war in Russia. The dedication of the drivers and the desperate urgency of their passage across the dark and lifeless desert was impressive. When silence and darkness had been restored we recommenced our progress, passed through Qum non-stop and arrived in a state of dust-laden fatigue outside the guardroom of the detention camp at Sultanabad at 10.00 p.m.

The guard sergeant appeared, a Royal Sussex man we instantly recognised, followed by several of his men, all Royal Sussex worthies, and our three prisoners clambered wearily out of the trucks. To my astonishment, guards and prisoners met each other with shouts of joy and fond embraces, the silent priest suddenly came to life and smiled broadly through his beard at one and all. Their luggage was unloaded and carried for them into the guardroom and hot tea and sustenance appeared by magic. 'Twas a Ritz Hotel welcome and no one paid any attention to the escort party who were left to fend for themselves. After shaking off the dust, we found a corner to lie in and fell asleep contemplating the return journey.

This commenced about 9.00 a.m. after we had scrounged some breakfast and, not fully recovered from the day before, I faced my ninth crossing of the miles of hot sand and salt lakes. The drivers drove as fast as vehicle suspensions would allow and in the rear we suffered an agonising bone-shaking seven-hour ordeal and arrived back in Teheran utterly exhausted. The following day was a Sunday and we were grateful for the opportunity to clean up and rest. 'In bed or out of barracks' was the established Army rule for Sundays but it was several days before we fully recovered. How many hours, I wondered, how many miles had I spent in the back of Army lorries? And how many more?

Cuckoo in the Mountains

October yielded to November and Teheran was growing cold. The Elburz Range was donning its winter coat of fresh clean snow and was starkly beautiful. The summer water supply for the city was assured for 1945. The thermometer dropped progressively as November passed and few were sorry when news was received of our imminent departure for the sunnier clime of Andimeshk, 300 miles south. Unusually, the battalion travelled by train which pleased one and all, especially those who had endured the recent escort journey across the desert.

On reaching Sultanabad we were surprised at the amount of snow on the peaks that far to the south and were unprepared for the chill in the mountains. The train became bitterly cold during the night and sleep was almost impossible. The train stopped at Do-roud in the early hours and we were up among the snow that lay thick on the platform. Andimeshk was reached by 10.00 a.m. and the snowy heights were behind us. A new camp awaited our occupation and I recalled our first arrival at Andimeshk when the camp was flattened during the night by the storm to end all storms and trusted lightning not to strike twice in the same place.

Andimeshk in November and December was less cold than Teheran but spells of wet and windy weather on the open plain were uncomfortably cold and the temperature fluctuated wildly. A 'Garrison Theatre' had been erected in the camp and an ambitious plan had been devised to stage a pantomime – *Dick Whittington and His Cat*. The cast was to be graced by lady volunteers from Teheran, mainly from the Embassy staff, and much practical assistance for stage properties, lighting and other technical aspects of theatrical productions was generously provided by American servicemen from Andimeshk. Pantomimes being so completely a British phenomenon, some of the Americans were puzzled by it

'Who is this guy Dick Whittington,' one asked me, 'is he one of your mob?'

After a traditional English Christmas much enjoyed by all, our traditional Boxing Day ended with the greatest ever production of *Dick Whittington and His Cat* that varied from the traditional in many ways. The ladies who had sacrificed so much of their Christmas to risk their lives as guests of the sergeants' mess for some days were hugely applauded. It was the next best thing to the family Christmas we just could not

139

have. Next year perhaps. Or the year after that.

At Andimeshk we were afforded the means of augmenting our often dreary cookhouse menu. A few miles away near a little habitation graced with the name of Shush was a region of small trees, shrubbery and thorns intersected by large ravines or gullies that ran to the Kharun river. The area was the home of wild pigs and pig-shooting parties of Sunday volunteers were organised. It was a strenuous exercise for we walked many miles, armed with our trusty Lee Enfield rifles, sometimes without seeing a pig all day. We had our successes however which entailed carrying our bag back to our transport which was not easy, but it was an enjoyable diversion. On one memorable occasion we formed a line and walked, like beaters at a pheasant shoot, along a wide ravine thick with bushes and scrub and a pig could be heard moving ahead. The pigs would often disappear and their tracks led into the river. The pig was suddenly seen in a clearing near the river bank. He was an old boar of formidable aspect with high bony shoulders, long ugly snout and great yellow tusks protruding from his dripping jaws. He apparently decided his swimming days were over and spun round and charged his pursuers.

In his path stood 'Ginger' Butcher who

had defied an enemy machine gun at Kidney Ridge. 'Ginger' was petrified. At the last moment he managed a nimble sidestep like a practised bullfighter and the old tusker brushed past his legs like an express train and was last heard crashing headlong through the bushes making his unlamented getaway.

The Sunday pig shoots ended abruptly when, while in the same ravine on a later date, we were startled by a burst of machine gun fire over our heads. The Americans from Andimeshk had moved in on our private sport with more sophisticated weaponry and neither we nor the unfortunate pigs were left with a sporting chance.

February 1945. The great struggle in Europe was raising the hopes of all that victory was just a matter of time, but British forces wherever they were stationed maintained a state of readiness. In the Middle East, hundreds of miles from the fighting with the desert battles seemingly years back in history, this was as true as anywhere. A training scheme had been organised for our battalion to prove we could move and operate in mountainous country without wheeled transport. After a night sleeping rough we commenced a long trek and the only transport in use were mules. What the mules did not carry, we did.

We had received training with these stubborn animals. We knew how to pack their loads, how to harness them, how to lead them, how to feed them. We had experienced some hilarious disasters in the process but we set off in the early morning full of hope. Everyone marched, cooks, clerks, drivers, everyone except the battalion commander who rode a horse. It was an exercise that would have appealed to General Montgomery's heart. Each one of us carried a heavy load with the same distinguished exception. The cooks with their stores and equipment and allotted mule-power set off very early to be able to prepare a meal for the main body on arrival at the appointed destination – a mere map reference number. The route to be followed was defined on the maps by a dotted line, a track none of us had trodden before. Its length was calculated but in the event the rigours of the march were underestimated.

The scenery was exciting. The track led along the brink of one dizzy precipice after another, up long steep inclines and down again and the temperature rose high under a clear sky. It soon became apparent that a dangerous situation was developing. The battalion column necessarily in single file was lengthening by the hour as the strongest strode resolutely on and the weaker fell behind. Those leading the mules soon found the mules were leading them. Should anyone have fallen by the wayside they would have been beyond the reach of wheeled transport, so, sore feet or not everyone trudged on. At one point on a steep ascent the track passed between two high rocks and the defile was too narrow for loaded mules. Each mule had to be unloaded and led through, its load manhandled and laboriously re-loaded.

It was a day of great exertion and endurance and the purpose of the Commanding Officer's horse became apparent as he trotted back and forth to keep watch over the leaders and the stragglers. His anxiety increased as light began to fail and the battalion was strung out over miles of mountain. The last in the line ran the risk of becoming lost in the darkness with no sustenance. Eventually, however, all reached the appointed spot safely and found the cooks with food and drink ready and as we settled on a grassy slope for the night our sweaty shirts became ice-cold. All was well that ended well but there was tomorrow. We had struggled along 20 miles and faced the same again.

Rising early with stiff and aching legs, we swallowed a hot breakfast, shouldered our loads and set forth once more. Many suffered sore feet and walked with their toes turned in and spoke little. The mountain air was clear and cold as we filed through the silent valleys between dramatic towering peaks. Suddenly there came a sound so completely unexpected, so reminiscent of home, everyone stopped to listen. It was a cuckoo.

The call came loud and clear in the breathless hush of a deep valley. The bird regaled us with its familiar notes bringing instant memories of English elms and oak woods, of copses in the summer time. No one took another step until the bird fell silent. It remained unseen but was the topic of conversation, for those with the energy to converse, for the remainder of the day. Though it did nothing for sore feet it was a great tonic for weary spirits. Some wag suggested that in the good old English tradition we should write to *The Times* to report hearing our first cuckoo on February 21st. 'Dear Editor – is this a record?'

Somehow we struggled through another 20 miles, somewhat less rigorous than the first, and spent our third night out trying to sleep in a cold wet shirt, and a few miles the next day brought us to the mountain road and the exercise was over. Motor transport arrived to return us to camp.

Many lessons were learned from it not the least being that our powers of endurance are always underestimated. 'You can do it if you try.' Also we were privileged to know where the cuckoos go for the winter months. Or at least one of them. Also, to some extent it gave us the lie to the often heard criticism that modern armies are road-bound, dependant on the internal combustion engine and much 'softer' than previous generations.

As we nursed our sore feet we hoped it would not be necessary to learn the lessons again. Once was enough. Roll on victory and let us go home. Victory, however, was still to be won though, by now, we did not expect to see enemy action again.

Modes of Travel

There was a tradition in the Middle East Command to hold a shooting match each year. This had been suspended during the war when shooting matches were in deadly earnest and the decision was made to revive the custom in 1945. The Middle East Rifle Meeting was duly arranged to be held near Cairo in April and invitations were sent to all units. The area within the Middle East Command was enormous, encompassing the vast area from Tripoli in Libya to Tripoli in Lebanon, to Teheran and the Persian Gulf, Aden and all Arabia. The event would attract some of the best riflemen of the day and our invitation was received with considerable misgiving because of the class of the competition. The challenge was accepted naturally for it amounted almost to a command. Not to take part would be shameful indeed, so the battalion organised its own elimination contest to select a team of six. Of all teams to compete there would be few with more distance to travel than ours. Egypt was about 1,600 miles away. It was an exciting prospect for the eventual team and a promise had been given that one week of leave would be allowed in Egypt after the meeting.

The elimination shoot was held on March 5th. Our squad of trained snipers were expected to excel in the contest and though I desperately wanted to travel to Cairo my performance was disappointing and at the end of the day I knew there were enough better shots than myself to form the team. My luck, however, had not deserted me. Because of the rigours of the journey it was considered advisable to send two reserves with the team and that secured my inclusion. Then began daily practise firing for almost three weeks.

Because of the huge list of entries for the various competitions our team could only be entered for one event. The actual time spent firing would be a few minutes for which we were to spend nearly two weeks travelling there and the same return journey after a week of leave, a total distance of approximately 3,000 miles. With hopes of plenty of opportunity to practise on the actual competition ranges before the event, our journey was planned to get us there one week early. Though we took the competition seriously, in itself the whole expensive excursion was regarded as a wonderful caper and we were all set to enjoy ourselves.

Boarding a train at Andimeshk on March 25th in the afternoon, we stopped at Ahwaz for the night. It was still hot enough there for flies to die. An early train next morning took us to a little station named Teneuma where we transferred to a narrow-gauge railway that was somewhat crude and devoid of comfort. The little fussy engine would emit high-pitched shrieks as it rattled on its rickety way across the Shatt-El-Arab to Margil, a suburb of Basra. The little train had a Walt Disney character about it and we were glad to leave it and move in for the night to a transit camp nearby.

Here we found a swimming pool and spent most of the next day waiting in it or by it till late afternoon when transport was provided to meet a train for Baghdad. As we approached the station we saw for the first time an example of one of the greatest plagues to contribute to the impoverishment of the Middle East. Locusts.

They were swarming all over Margil and appeared to be very poor fliers for they were crashing into anything that stood in their way. There were locusts crawling in the street, crashing into buildings and creeping over our truck. Small Arab boys were hitting them down with sticks and eating portions of their anatomy. At the station the platforms, the tracks and the trains were all festooned with crawling locusts that had crash-landed and were instinctively trying to move on with the swarm. In the sky they flew with the wind as thick as snowflakes in a blizzard.

We were back with Walt Disney. Leaving Margil at 6.30 p.m. with locusts crawling all over the train, we bumped and clattered our way into the night. There was gross over-crowding and attempting to sleep sitting up on hard wooden seats was not very restful. The train rocked and jerked without mercy and fine dust was filtering in through every crack and window and a very rough time was had by all.

The rigours of the journey were relieved by a pleasant interlude that occurred as we approached Baghdad. A number of American servicemen were travelling on the train and in the course of a conversation with one of them it emerged he was a train driver plying up and down the Iranian railway and he told us how he had waited at Khorramshahr for two weeks with a special train to take Winston Churchill to the Teheran conference. It was a delightful coincidence and his pleasure at meeting one of the escort party was expressed with typical American generosity. Rummaging among his kit he produced a snapshot of an Iranian train passing along a typically barren stretch of line and wrote his name and address on the back.

Wilson C. Leppert lived in Painsville, Ohio, and he said, 'If you are ever in Painsville, just drop in.'

The Teheran conference was already history but such gatherings of the mighty touch the lives of many lesser mortals and both Wilson C. Leppert and myself were still suffering a degree of disappointment over the journey that might have been. The train arrived at Baghdad at 1.00 p.m. we were soon once more in Lancer camp.

The next stage of our travel was familiar to us by now but the mode of travel was unique. We were going by bus. Damascus was 550 miles away and it was the most unlikely bus service imaginable. Nairn Transport was a company formed by a New Zealander reputed to have been 'left over' from the First World War who saw a need and set out to fill it. The bus, American built, waited for us at Lancer Camp. It was a single-decked articulated vehicle capable of carrying 40 passengers and their luggage. There were two Iraqi drivers. While one drove his companion slept among the luggage.

Before leaving Baghdad we spent a restful day in Lancer Camp and revisited the old city, never being quite sure if we would ever see it again. Boarding the bus next day and luxuriating in its sumptuous upholstery, we moved grandly out of camp and hit the high road for Damascus at 5.00 p.m. We were travelling in style, no expense spared. The bus route to Damascus was not quite the same as the Army convoys used. The first stop was at the Habbaniya Royal Air Force base where passengers were put down. From there the bus found its way to Ramadi, a little town with an hotel where a good dinner was provided for us late at night.

Darkness brought the natural desire to sleep, the same desire that drives a pheasant into a tree, where it sleeps peacefully. Riding on a bus it is grotesquely difficult. Some of the passengers succeeded. There are always those who can sleep whatever the circumstances. At least when travelling by lorry convoy we always stopped for the night and slept even if it was underneath the lorry itself. Our Nairn bus paid no heed to darkness and it reached the lonesome town of Rutbah at 3.00 a.m. and surprise, surprise, pulled up at a N.A.A.F.I. canteen that was open and waiting for us.

After Rutbah this remarkable bus left the road and followed its own route across the desert. The surface was dusty and at times uneven and the bus rocked and swayed through the darkness. Daylight revealed the great Syrian desert with no road, no pipeline or telegraph line. The track had a few marker posts but at times it seemed the driver's navigation was that of a homing pigeon. Dust billowed up and ran down the windows like dirty water. Everyone was tired, unshaven and uncomfortable after all night in the bus and the 'style' of our travel had deteriorated.

To my mind our arrival at Damascus equated with the *Santa Rosa* arriving at Freetown harbour after two weeks at sea. A triumph of navigation. At 4.00 p.m. we disembarked in the transit camp after a 23-hour bus ride. Travelling by lorry convoy in June 1944 to reach Damascus from Baghdad occupied five days.

April 1st was a Sunday. A day of rest and an opportunity to visit the most ancient of cities and walk in the presence of history. Damascus was inhabited by man before he kept records. In the seventh century B.C. it was the capital of the civilised world. It was the city of Saul of Tarsus, where he was cured of his blindness. The Street called Straight was still there. Architectural evidence of Greek and Roman occupations could be seen in its arches and columns. Damascus is more durable than time. Men come to the city, make their mark and pass on. Damascus remains to remind man of his limited span on this sphere and he leaves its ancient walls a wiser and more humble being.

The unforgettable Nairn bus had left us. Our next 'hop' was by narrow gauge rail again. A fascinating way to cross the fertile acres of Syria and new country for our party as we neared Deraa on the heights above Palestine. The train lingered at Deraa long enough for us to have dinner there.

There followed the most colourful and picturesque journey one could dream of as the little rail led the train down towards Galilee. On the one side the hills and even the narrow ledge carrying the rails were covered in grasses and wild flowers, while on the other was a sheer drop to a racing turbulent river below. Beyond the river the hills rose precipitous and beautiful forming a deep valley leading down to Galilee, that was a floral delight for travellers. Rattling away downhill the heights seemed to grow and the narrow river come nearer. Looking forward I saw a narrow spider's web of a bridge spanning the river far below it and the train turned on to it following an incredibly tight turn in the rails, causing the wheels to grind ominously and the little carriages to lurch and shudder. Crossing the bridge, all that could be seen of it from a passenger's viewpoint was a shadow on the tumbling waters below.

Stopped at a halt on the way down, there was a pause for a goods train labouring up from Tiberias loaded with oranges in bulk. The delicious aroma of fresh fruit came up with it and filled the valley. The line cleared by its passing, our little engine steamed onwards and at a lower level was delayed by a dozen goats grazing on the ledge. Angrily the driver banged his fist on the side of his cabin and one by one the goats stepped off the rails and teetered perilously on the brink of the abyss while the train steamed slowly by. After the most delightful stretch of rail travel I ever hope to enjoy we arrived in Tiberias station with a glimpse of the sea of Galilee on our right.

The whole station and its goods sidings smelt only of oranges. The goods trains seemed to carry nothing else. Oranges were spilt everywhere. Moving on towards Haifa, the train treated us to a view of Palestine's rural plenty. Miles of flat productive farmland reeled by and as we approached a level crossing a group of people waved to the driver who dutifully stopped the train to allow them to climb aboard. The waiting passengers included an Arab woman with a calf which, with a little help, was persuaded to travel by rail. Perhaps it was market day in Haifa. It was a delightful little railway.

Journey's end for the day was a transit camp in Haifa with sound buildings, good sound beds, the Mediterranean sea on one side and Mount Carmel on the other. No travel had been arranged for the next day so we were able to visit Haifa. Whatever happened at the rifle meeting we were enjoying the journey to it. The town was dominated by its waterfront and it bustled with noisy activity. There were many very modern buildings and broad thoroughfares that contrasted starkly with its ancient origins. The sea inevitably aroused old desires to set sail across it and return to our native shores. This desire for home was growing apace in all of us. Migratory birds respond to it by spreading their wings.

Wednesday April 4th saw us bidding farewell to Haifa in mid afternoon as we boarded the train, a full-sized normal gauge train, for Cairo. The coaches seemed huge and luxurious after the little trains we had patronised and it rolled in full majesty through the orange groves, stopping at Lydda and Gaza as darkness descended and we contemplated how to snatch a little sleep. There were so many passengers, room to 'stretch out' was at a premium. Our coach contained a number of young Palestinian sailors. Palestine was still British Mandated territory and boasted a navy with a gunboat or two. They too, desired to sleep and unpacked their hammocks and strung them across the coach hung on the luggage racks. Some lay on the luggage racks and others in the central corridor. British servicemen, not being equipped with hammocks, curled up on the floor or on the seats or joined the Palestinians on the luggage racks which were grossly overloaded. Some of us formed a 'card school' and played into the early hours with hammocks swinging heavily over our heads. A good soldier, it is said, does not stand up when he can sit down and only sits down when unable to lie down. The Haifa to Cairo train as it rumbled across the Sinai desert during the darkest hours was full of such good soldiers.

The onset of dawn provided a diversion that was bizarre.

Two Military Policemen appeared through the door at one end of the coach and shouted, in voices designed to wake the dead, 'Come on, let's have you – baggage search.'

Despite a chorus of indignant protests, they stepped between the kitbags and sleeping bodies, shaking one and all to rouse them. It was the Palestinians they were seeking. They were compelled to turn out of their hammocks or off the luggage racks and empty their kitbags. Proof of British nationality gave immunity from a search but not to being trodden on or partly buried in Palestinian undergarments. The Redcaps were searching for hashish. They worked their way through the coach and disappeared without finding any and the scene they left behind them was like a mad hallucination.

The train halted at Kantara. It was April 5th and we were back in Egypt. Along the canal, across it to Ismailia – it was almost a homecoming after two years away. We rolled smoothly into Cairo at 9.15 a.m. and transport was waiting to convey us to Abbassia Barracks.

Holidays and Memories

It was strange to be in barracks, after roughing it for so long under canvas or under the stars. There was an atmosphere of security and permanence that was reminiscent of Devizes Barracks which I remembered vacating with hundreds of other recruits nearly five years ago to make room for the influx from the Dunkirk beaches. We soon settled in but were here far too soon. The rifle ranges were not ready for practice firing so there was virtually nothing for us to do

156

for over a week except visit Cairo and amuse ourselves as we wished. Those of us who had opted to spend our week of leave in Alexandria were delighted to have a week in Cairo as a bonus.

A visit to the Pyramids and the Sphynx was a natural diversion for one day, and from there a glimpse of the old desert of 1942. The 'blue'. Memories flooded back. Alam Haifa and Kidney Ridge were only 70 miles away. All silent now, the great crashing of artillery, the screaming Stukas, the countless personal dramas of thousands of individuals, all a thing of the past. Time had indeed, like an ever-rolling stream, borne all its sons away and the desert had reclaimed its peace and solitude. The Sphynx gazed across the wilderness as it always did as though nothing had happened. I could almost convince myself nothing had. If only I could, just for a few minutes, stand on Alam Halfa ridge and gaze across to Himeimat where it all started for me! I returned to Cairo and dismissed such daydreams from my mind. Why should any sane person wish to return to such a fly-blown spot?

A special camp had been prepared at Maadi, a Cairo suburb, for the Middle East Rifle Meeting. On April 16th we moved in and devoted the following day to 'getting our eye in' and our team event was held on April 18th. All our men were fit and well so, as a team reserve, I was wholly unnecessary and could enjoy the role of spectator. There were 48 teams competing in the event and the Royal Sussex team gained eighth place. It was a good result and all concerned were well pleased and on April 21st we dispersed for our leave and those bound for Alexandria caught the noon train from Cairo.

There was a small guest house in Alexandria named Gloucester House. Run by a Greek family, the name was, no doubt, chosen to attract the British serviceman on leave. Four of us booked in there and were well catered for at a very reasonable cost. There were sights to see in Alexandria. The broad sweep of the promenade skirting the harbour was a great attraction for those with time to dawdle in the sunshine and the beautiful Antoniades Gardens provided a refuge from the noisy city streets. We joined a conducted tour of one of King Farouk's palatial residences. There was a burly Australian serviceman in the party who expressed great interest in Queen Farida's bedroom. The Royal bed was large and circular in shape and he draped his irreverent form across it and said he would wait for her to come home. We dissociated ourselves from him completely and dutifully followed our embarrassed guide as he showed us where Winston Churchill slept when he visited the Eighth Army in 1942. We were on Alam Halfa ridge at the time sleeping in rather less opulent quarters. Alexandria was rich in antiques. The ancient catacombs and the great red granite obelisk, 80 feet high and weighing 200 tons and known as 'Pompey's Pillar', were there to interest 'foreign tourists' such as ourselves.

Our leave expired on May Day and we returned to Cairo by train and the Royal Sussex rifle team were reunited in Abbassia Barracks. The time had come to leave Egypt once more to travel all the long way back to rejoin the battalion in Iran. There was a great wild hope rising within us. The war in Europe was surely near its end. Radio news bulletins were given rapt attention. English language newspapers were read and read again. We dared to think of home but there was still Japan to reckon with. In the meantime the only possible philosophy was to 'soldier on'.

Victory Celebrations

With the Third Reich falling apart at the seams, revealing its terrible inner secrets to a horror-sated world, the Royal Sussex rifle team left Cairo on the 6.00 p.m. train for Haifa. Another nocturnal ride across the

Sinai in somewhat better style. No sailors' hammocks strung across the coach and no dawn baggage search. Reaching Haifa by noon, we returned to the transit camp on the seashore. Tomorrow would be a lovely day spent on the little train chuffing its way to Galilee and up between the soaring hills among the flowers and the goats. Till then there was a whole afternoon to while away visiting Haifa and contemplating the future.

The war against Germany was very near its end, a thought so tremendous in its implications it was difficult to accept. What of Japan? They would fight on in their fanatical way. There would be a dreadful slaughter there before it was over, on both sides. What of ourselves? Questions, many questions. But no answers.

Leaving Haifa next morning, our favourite little train fussed its way across the Palestinian farmland into Tiberias and laboured manfully up the unforgettable heights into Syria. From Derea onwards the journey presented us with a sight such as I never thought to see. A sight I had read of but could never have pictured in my mind. A locust swarm of massive proportions. We had been introduced to these ravaging insects in Margil while on our way to Cairo but we were now in open farmland and as far as the eye could see in any direction including upwards were millions of locusts. They covered the entire landscape, crawling, eating and flying off with strings of excreta hanging from their rears. The train ran along a shallow embankment that was green with crawling crashing insects. They rose in front of the engine like a bow wave in front of a ship. They struck the train windows and slithered down the glass. An Arab farmer was on his knees in prayer with locusts all over and around him. It was a tremendous and tragic sight. The train ploughed through them for miles before there came any break in the green cloud. Then we travelled through intermittent swarms all the way to Damascus. As we walked along the platform we observed the sturdy little engine. There were dead and dying locusts all over it. In every metal nook and cranny the corpses were lodged with the still living crawling over them and falling to the track.

How blessed, I thought, are the British Isles! The farmer at home could complain about rabbits, about the voracious wood pigeons and ravaging rooks. At least he could shoot them, trap them, destroy their nests. He could always put a ferret down a rabbit hole and net himself a dinner. What would he say to millions of locusts on his spring barley? He could neither shoot them, trap them, or destroy their nests. He could only emulate the Arab farmer we had seen earlier.

No travelling on the morrow. 'Twas a

Sunday. It was 'in bed or out of barracks' or in the swimming pool. Monday midday brought back the Nairn bus.

The same two drivers manned the bus which was reassuring for we trusted their navigation. A midday start and we were well into the desert as darkness fell. Sleep was doubly hard to come by now there was so much of importance to think about. All that had passed. All that was about to happen. When would we hear the great news? At Rutbah in the early hours of May 8th the N.A.A.F.I. canteen was open for the proverbial 'tea and wads'. On the way again and the whole busload were utterly weary, unwashed and unshaven. The hotel at Ramadi provided us with a 10.00 a.m. breakfast. The Iraqi proprietor was talking excitedly in disjointed English and pointing to a radio set.

'Finish,' he said. 'All Finish.'

We chose to ignore him. Until such time we heard the news in good English with at least an air of authority the war was still on. Our indifference left him quite bewildered. The next stop was the Royal Air Force station, Habbaniya. We arrived there in various grotesque attitudes of sleep and were feeling quite wretched.

A Royal Air Force sergeant, commander of the guard on the main gate boarded the bus.

'This is official,' he announced, 'the war with Germany is over. I thought you would be glad to know.'

His dramatic gesture fell absolutely flat. For years we had lived for and dreamed of this wonderful news item. Thousands, millions, had died to achieve the victory and we were all so tired and hot and uncomfortable the only comment to emerge was an ungracious 'about time too'. I would have thrown my hat in the air at least, but not on a bus. The sergeant of the guard left the bus and returned to his guardroom rather crestfallen. If he could have read our minds he would have known just how profound the effect of his message really was. We confined ourselves to our private thoughts. Baghdad lay ahead of us. There could be high jinks in Lancer Camp, I thought. Celebrations and thanksgiving after a wash and brush-up would be in order.

Alighting from Nairn Transport at 1.30 p.m. the temperature was 108 degrees Fahrenheit. We dragged ourselves into our quarters and set to work reviving ourselves and smartening up to look more like members of the winning side. A radio set was found somewhere and a crowd gathered round to listen to King George VI. He spoke of his troops in far-flung outposts. That was us, we all agreed, and one cynic remarked that this far-flung outpost had not been flung far enough.

Terrible news was coming from Europe. Belsen, Auschwitz, Buchenwald, Ravensbruck. Names that raised a shudder in all who heard them. Place names that made one ashamed of the human race, ashamed to be of the generation that committed such crimes against God and humanity.

'Who could do these things?'

'What sort of people were they?'

The question begged an answer. My thoughts ranged back to my brief encounter with the war. I knew I had seen the answer, before I heard the question. The answer was in the face of the young blond blue-eyed prisoner from Kidney Ridge, whose blood stained the desert sand. In that face so devoid of human feelings, so set in a mould of hatred and towering arrogance. He and his kind were beaten at last and somehow the German nation would rise and cleanse itself. A religious service of thanksgiving was attended by all who could. There was much to be thankful for. It was too hot for high jinks.

Rejoining the Walt Disney railway at 6.30 p.m. next evening we journeyed through the night. There were few passengers so there was room to sleep on the seats or on the floor. Margil was like an oven. The air hung hot and heavy and the camp swimming pool was the only place to live. Lingering at

Margil for two days, we were driven to Teneuma on May 13th and reunited with the Iranian railway which duly deposited us in Ahwaz which was still steaming hot. The next day Andimeshk hove into view about midday and the slow laborious climb into the mountains was as thrilling as ever. It was always a different journey, a succession of surprises.

The battalion had moved into the mountains while we were capering up and down the Nile Valley and we found them at Do-roud. It was a muddy little camp near the station. It had been raining again. There was an accumulation of mail from home to greet me, most of it posted five or six weeks previously. Stepping back into normal Army routine was not easy. We had been away for seven weeks and had travelled about 3,500 miles for a few minutes' shooting and we had enjoyed a great experience. Do-roud was high in the mountains, the scenery was majestic and being near the railway we often heard the supply trains rumbling through the night while doing our stint of sentry duty. The big throbbing diesels ruled the rails hauling huge loads, for the end of the war in Europe did not automatically stop the flow. Occasionally the undulating moaning whistle from an old steam locomotive would be heard among the peaks reminding me always of my first encounter with the railways of Iran.

The battalion split temporarily on June 30th when my company moved by road to Sultanabad. A great improvement for us. We were accommodated in sound buildings and very close to the town. Midsummer in Sultanabad was sultry and dusty and there was one depressing aspect of our new abode. The town was one side of us, and a graveyard the other side and it was not so much the life of Sultanabad that passed before our eyes as the mortal remains of life past. Each day there were sad little processions passing our main gate and the dead were so often small children or babies carried under a sheet in the arms of a grieving father with the sobbing mother following behind with a small group of wailing relatives. After the burial the sorrowing family would return home and in the evening the women would return to the graveside and wail and lament in great distress. Child mortality must have been at a very high level in the intense heat of July for the funeral processions were frequent.

The reuniting of the battalion took place on July 23rd as we boarded a train carrying the other companies from Do-roud and we travelled yet again to Teheran. Once again across the Qum desert, for me the eleventh time, but most of it in darkness and during sleep. We were becoming proficient at sleeping in trains that do not cater for sleep. Teheran hove into view by 6.30 a.m. and we were soon back into our former camp.

High summer in Teheran meant a daily temperature around 90 degrees Fahrenheit. Demavend had retained its cap of snow but the lesser heights of the Elburz range were revealed in their rugged grandeur. Battalion life settled into an easy routine. Some of the urgency had gone from our existence. Occasional outings were arranged to a fashionable suburb named Darband. It was a beautiful spot with a huge semi-natural swimming pool set among tall trees with enough space around it to play cricket on sweet soft grass.

Meanwhile the shooting war continued. Germany lay in ruins and the world looked towards Japan and held its breath. It was now an accepted belief that we would not be sent to the Far East. Our period of foreign service was too far advanced. If we moved anywhere it would be towards home. But when? There was a joke going the rounds. 'They were building a boat specially for us at Port Said but the locals had stolen the rivets.'

The issue was settled for us by news of shattering impact. The Atomic Bomb. Whatever has been said since there is no doubting one point. It was greeted as the best news we had heard in years. The repercussions of

167

the Hiroshima and Nagasaki shock waves were unassessable. Only one thing mattered. Japan was beaten. To have defeated the Japanese by conventional means would have been at a frightful cost in lives and suffering on both sides of the conflict. So we rejoiced in our hearts.

August 15th was V.J. day and the battalion was paraded before the Medical Officer and lectured very firmly about V.D. It had been pre-arranged and no little matter like an atom bomb or two could be allowed to disrupt anything so vital. I felt cheated. V.E. day was such a disappointment on the Nairn bus and now V.J. day was being robbed of its joy by the Medical Officer telling us little we were not already aware of.

In despair, a party of us visited Teheran in the evening and found it bedecked in British, American, Iranian and Russian flags. It was heartening to see all the various flags fluttering in the same breeze. Would the world live up to the symbolism? We drank quietly together and talked of going home. There seemed to be no good reason for staying.

A service of Thanksgiving was held on Sunday August 19th. We marched to the British Embassy and entered its sacred precincts. The service was a moving occasion and the British Ambassador, Sir Reader Bullard, addressed the parade. The following Tuesday and Wednesday were declared a holiday but it was not till September 12th that the Royal Sussex left Teheran permanently. This time we had no doubts. A lot of equipment and stores had been crated up and the magic words 'NOT WANTED ON VOYAGE' stencilled thereon. We were homeward bound. There was a long way to go. Little did we know how long it would take.

Homeward Bound

When the wheels started to roll at 8.00 a.m. I breathed a private prayer of thanksgiving. Having said farewell to Merseyside on May 31st 1942 I was eager to do likewise to Teheran. It had all been a wonderful experience but the call of my native land was now a constant inner ache. The yearn to re-enter the family fold and divest myself of military trappings was becoming overpowering.

Our convoy detoured through the streets as a farewell gesture. The bustling business of everyday living was already in full swing and as urgent as ever. Little attention was paid to us but I welcomed the opportunity for a final glimpse of the pavements I had pounded for so long. Perhaps it was also as a gesture that those in command had chosen a detour avoiding the eternal Qum desert. The column headed north-west for Kazvin and there were a few of us who could remember how rough that stretch of road was. Even without a hangover it was an ordeal but what did it matter. 'Twas one way home.

After Kazvin the road surface improved and our route brought us to Takistan where we stopped for the night. A high wind was blowing and, lying on the ground wrapped in a blanket, sleep was difficult. We shivered all night with only the prospect of home to warm us. Moving in a south-westerly course, we headed for Hamadan 126 miles on. There was a road accident in Hamadan when one of our vehicles struck an Iranian woman who was in the street with her child. The unfortunate mother suffered a broken leg. There was a delay of some hours while all possible help was given. The tragedy of the incident was deeply felt. For such a thing to happen during our last hours in the country was a cause of heartfelt regret.

The strong winds still blew through our second cold night and we were glad to be driving south. From Hamadan there was a long climb through mountains via the Shah Pass, the highest road in Iran. An impressive climb but lacking the thrills of the Pai-tak Pass which we would descend on the morrow. The end of the day saw us in familiar country once more as we approached Kermanshah. The wind still blew harshly as though to hasten our departure and another chilly night was spent on the ground with dust blowing all around us.

Iran withdrew into the distance and from our lives as we crossed the Iraqi plain after descending the Pai-tak Pass which again exercised its power to heighten the heart-beat. A night stop at Kahnaqin was an opportunity to look back on the distant Zagros range and see them as I first saw them in 1943. They were as mysterious and inviting in their purple remoteness as before. I felt I knew something of what they protected. Something perhaps only a little, but enough to know that one does not live and breathe with the Middle Eastern peoples without some changes within one-self. A little more wisdom perhaps, a great deal more tolerance and a degree of humility.

Back in Baghdad next day and still there two days later. We always lingered in Baghdad. It was a sort of hot half-way house and even Army trucks need a rest. From Baghdad it was the familiar long flat dead-straight road. Rutbah, H.4, Mafraq, a road four days long. Across Jordan and down and down into the Jordan Valley below the level of the sea. Palestine was kind to the eyes and

171

from on high it presented a picturesque panorama. Now it seemed we really were homeward bound.

After pausing for a day near Nathaniel we passed again through a land of abundance. A land flowing with milk and honey and on into harsh rocky barrenness to Beersheba. Resting awhile some of us visited the First War military cemetery. Memories of the Mesopotamia of our forefathers. Australian graves and, we were touched to find, Royal Sussex graves in neat and well-tended order, giving a silent reminder of yesteryear. First War trenches were nearby, silent now and pregnant with spiritual presence. Testimony of man's failings. Trenches and graves.

On through the Negev desert we spent the night on the fringes of Sinai and an early start took us to the Eastern bank of the Suez Canal by evening with sufficient time for a swim in its welcoming waters. Approaching the canal from the desert it is unseen between its banks and we enjoyed the spectacle of a merchant ship apparently sailing through the desert. In the morning we reached Kantara bridge and found it swung open to permit passage of an English cargo ship. There was an exchange of good-natured banter with some crewmen on deck. The vessel was sailing the wrong way or we would have been tempted to jump aboard.

After crossing the canal we headed for Suez itself whereas we would have preferred Port Said as the obvious port to catch a boat home.

Suez it was, or within two miles of it. Back under canvas once more on sandy desert. Then the news was broken to us. There was no ship available for us.

'I told you so,' a cynic remarked, 'they really have pinched the rivets.'

There was the best of all reasons for the shortage of shipping. The situation was explained and though by now we were all suffering the onset of acute homesickness, the facts were accepted without a word or gesture of complaint.

Prisoners of war, recently released from a barbarous captivity in the Far East, were being given absolute priority for shipment home. Large passenger vessels were bringing them to Suez where they were transferred to smaller ships that could negotiate the Canal. A transit camp had been erected near Port Tewfiq, the port area of Suez, and men from our battalion were there daily to lend what assistance they could. They returned with horrific tales of the condition of many of the ex-prisoners and greatest irony of all was the account of a victim dying in the camp. To have survived such horrors and die on the homeward passage was so desperately sad that the bearer of the news found difficulty in speaking so intense was his grief and anger.

The world was being shaken by the horrors and bestiality of the war now it was over. The extermination camps, the Burma railway, Changi gaol – and the Atomic Bomb – all evidence of a trait in human nature that left the mind in pain. How little some of us knew about it all. How fortunate my worthy colleagues and I had been. The war for me had been a tremendous experience. On reflection it all seemed unfair. Some suffered so terribly, some not at all. Being helpless to remedy the situation was not enough. There was an inner fear that the need for thankfulness and gratitude would be soon forgotten. At least we could stay at Suez for as long as need be and never grumble again.

Our stay in Egypt was far more prolonged than expected. Back in the United Kingdom the demobilisation process was under way. Demobilisation – the most attractive word in the English language. Those among us who qualified by age and length of service were duly found space in a homeward-bound vessel and we watched them leave camp with envious eyes. We were leading a leisurely life at Suez. There were plenty of opportunities for swimming in Suez bay and other entertainment was available but the desire to sail home grew stronger as time passed without any hint of when it would be fulfilled. Christmas came and was celebrated in traditional fashion though it was a Christmas we had hoped to spend with our families.

Immediately after the festive season I joined a leave party for Alexandria. We booked ourselves in at Gloucester House as before. The Royal Navy allowed soldiers on leave to enjoy the facilities of the Fleet Club where a sumptuous meal could be enjoyed in sumptuous surroundings. The great attraction of the Fleet Club was the amateur talent contests held in the beer garden. The beer flowed in large volume and the talent ranged from passable to downright appalling. This hilarious event was styled *The Sailors' Opera*. It was free. It was priceless. A sunshine stroll along the promenade round the East Harbour revealed a scale model of a Roman Galleon floating on the still waters where a film company was working on the production of *Cleopatra*.

The leave lasted one enjoyable week and we were grateful for the hospitality of the Royal Navy. On January 5th we boarded a train and left for Suez. Changing trains at Ben-ha, we arrived at Ismailia and returned to camp by road. Demobilisation parties were still leaving us and we who remained consoled each other with the certain knowledge that 'it cannot be long now'.

An official statement was eventually issued on January 14th containing the long-awaited news.

'The battalion will be returning to the United Kingdom shortly.'

The next two weeks dragged by agonisingly slowly. Final packing began on the 28th. It did not take long. Little had been unpacked since leaving Teheran in September. So it came to pass that on Wednesday January 30th we shouldered our kit and all our accoutrements and boarded another train. We were off. The train ran alongside the canal as it headed for Port Said. The French battleship *Richelieu* was steaming through bringing to mind the unhappy days of 1940, the days of Vichy France, when she was attacked and disabled in the harbour at Dakar by a Royal Navy motor boat and Fleet Air Arm torpedo bombers. She was so new then she had not been commissioned. Her birth had been a painful one but she had survived and for a short while we travelled alongside each other in the same homeward direction. The aircraft carrier *Indomitable* was also negotiating the Canal and we were reminded that though the war had been over five months we were not the only exiles left in foreign climes. As the train clattered over the points on reaching Port Said our eyes searched the quays for a likely troop carrier.

'There she is,' someone yelled and eager arms pointed her out.

There she was indeed, complete with all her rivets. Despite her war paint our biased eyes credited her with a great beauty. The Union Castle liner *Dunottar Castle* was a pleasure to behold. There were many passengers already aboard and we soon joined them and settled into our quarters. There was ample space for all and hammocks had been provided for our use. Having dumped our kit, we mingled with the other passengers on deck. It was a cosmopolitan gathering. Civilians, men and women, mixed with soldiers, sailors, airmen, merchant seamen and service nurses. Everyone was happy and all decks were open to everyone.

Returning to our quarters, we set about mastering the hammocks. As a mode of slumber it was foreign to us but if the Palestinian sailors could use them on a train we could surely manage somehow. Hanging them on the rails provided was simple enough even without a maritime knowledge of knots. The difficulty was getting in and out without disaster. Once in they were indeed very comfortable though any movement called for care. With a lot of good-humoured banter we all eventually hung from the ceiling like a colony of bats and drifted into sleep with lovely thoughts of home and the coming pleasures of a Mediterranean cruise. Tomorrow we would say our farewells to the Middle East.

To Sussex by the Sea

There was a general desire to be astir early next morning. It would be unforgivable to be asleep as the ship sailed and she moved early. At 6.00 a.m. the gap between her hull and the quay widened and she was gently nudged away into wider waters. After a quick breakfast I leaned on the stern rail to see Egypt slowly slip away into the past.

It was a very private experience. I recalled watching Liverpool and Birkenhead fade away from the stern of the *Santa Rosa* nearly four years previously wondering what the future held. So much had happened that would be forever in my memory. The sum total of it all was the effect it had had upon me. Outwardly a little older. Inwardly a different person, having seen something more of God's creation and of his peoples. The war had been won, but war was the product of evil. It revealed how thin is the veneer of civilisation and what animal savagery can be unleashed when its restraining influences are cast aside. There was also surely some lasting good to be derived from it. Races were forced to mix and live together which could only help to dispel the ignorance and greed and intolerance that bred war. Perhaps now we could be at peace with our former enemies in life as well as in Mersa Matruh cemetery. I was conscious of a lasting regard for the peoples of the Middle Eastern lands, living in a world so different from our own. They have much to teach Western man. They are, above all, a religious people. Perhaps this comes from the spiritual impact of the vast deserts. Their environment being so empty, their spiritual nature is free to sustain them in the manner of a priest finding spiritual revival in a monastic retreat.

The last distant smudge of land disappeared over the hazy horizon and the moving deck swung my thoughts back to the moment. To mingle in a leisurely fashion with so many people in the warm sunshine surrounded by the blue placid sea was a taste of paradise. The *Dunottar Castle* sailed with full majesty cutting a bow wave of impeccable colour and leaving a foaming wake far back into the past. I savoured the moment with an inner sensation of contentment and gratitude.

With the coming of eventide the ship was a blaze of lights. Somehow this came as a surprise. The need for concealment was gone. The war really was over. There was an atmosphere of carnival. The darkness was warm, balmy and the lights illuminated the dark waters that were bearing us home. The past was gone. The future could wait. This voyage was to be enjoyed as no other voyage I might undertake ever could be. Time came to go to roost in our tricky hammocks. I turned in reluctantly for sleep puts an end to happy thoughts.

Rolling out of the hammocks next morning our feet encountered a deck that was moving more than expected. A viewing through a porthole revealed a choppy sea that heaved quite strongly. Stepping on to the open deck, the wind struck with rude force. The Mediterranean was about to show us the Atlantic has no monopoly in rough sailing conditions. The wind grew stronger by the hour and the *Dunottar Castle* pitched and rolled and her metal belly – groaned and creaked in protest as she struggled resolutely through the great walls of water that threatened her. It was exciting to watch as her stern seemed about to sink for ever only to soar up into the sky as the bows dived into foaming rollers that slammed into her forward plates and swirled across her foredeck.

Darkness heightened the dramatic quality of the scene as the deck lights shone on the watery hills as they advanced behind a screen of flying rain and slid beneath her keel and reappeared roaring upwards on the other side. There were many whose stomachs rebelled at the ceaseless motion of the deck but what did it matter? We were sailing home. The good ship *Dunottar Castle* steamed steadily on into the darkness as we returned to our hammock-borne slumbers and I could appreciate why sailors love their ships.

The Mediterranean repented of its waywardness and granted us a warm and pleasant day to follow the storm. The contortions of the sea had subsided to a gentle swell and the sun shone warm and gracious as we approached Malta. Another passenger liner appeared astern on the starboard side and as the day progressed she gradually drew level and eventually disappeared ahead but the *Dunottar Castle* only desired to give her passengers a voyage of pleasure rather than speed and who was in a hurry? We were homeward bound. Nothing else mattered.

The sea had achieved a state of blissful calm next morning and at 11.00 a.m. we sailed triumphantly into Valletta harbour. The anchor chains chattered as the *Dunottar Castle* proclaimed to the world she had come to rest awhile. There was no chance for us to go ashore but the view from the deck was enthralling. Here it was. The

George Cross island. Battered but un-bowed. A huge mass of fissured rock from which Valletta had been carved, glowing warm in the sunshine. A beautiful natural harbour resting quietly in the sunny glow of peace.

Malta was slipping away from us as we gingerly descended from our hammocks on the morn of February 4th and Sicily loomed large on the port side. The colossus of Mount Etna rose to the heavens in a mantle of snow emitting a plume of smoke from its lofty mouth. Etna like ourselves was at peace with the world but it breathed a threat to all who dwelt on its capacious slopes. On the starboard side the famous 'toe' of Italy reached out to see who was coming and we steamed through the Straits of Messina as darkness fell.

With lights fully on, other people's houses always appear inviting to the passing stranger and as the *Dunottar Castle* headed away from the Messina narrows into the wide empty darkness of the sea the receding shores of Italy and Sicily were twinkling with well-lit hearths and homes that beckoned an invitation to stay for the night. However the happy ship forged on into the regions of darkness for she had other sights to show us.

Late at night I heard a sudden yell from the port side rail.

'Come and look at this!'

For a moment I disbelieved my own eyes. High in the blackness of the night sky was a great glowing ball of angry red light colouring a billowing cloud of smoke. A flaming red stream was flowing from it in an angled descent to the sea. It was like something from Hell's inferno. As we gathered to watch there came the same repeated question.

'Whatever is it?'

The answer came from somewhere. It was the volcano Stromboli erupting into the night and it was a spectacle no one could resist. The conical shape of the volcano could be dimly discerned as we approached. The fire from its lofty vent periodically diminished only to suddenly blaze forth as if the Devil himself was stoking its internal furnace. The lava stream glowed and flared as it slowly slid down the steep incline to the unseen waters below. As Mother Nature's firework display receded into the distance we retired late after an exhilarating day.

Waking early, lest we miss something, a quick dash on deck revealed a scene of natural splendour. The good ship *Dunottar Castle* was in the Bay of Naples. Shrouded in mist was Mount Vesuvius. Bathed in sunshine was Capri and ahead of us lay Naples and its dockland and a berth awaited our arrival.

Surrounding us was the wreckage of war.

Huge dockside buildings lay in ruins, wrecked cranes lay where they fell in tangled impotence and a small ship sat grotesquely with its stern leaning on the quayside and its bows under the dockland water. A massive task of rebuilding awaited the Italians but such thoughts were for the future. The Naples' dock area epitomised the state of all the European nations so recently released from war. Battered, wounded and weary, pausing awhile till the blood of renewed life pumped through its veins once more and bodily strength was restored. There was much shipping in the harbour but little life on the quayside but the *Dunottar Castle* collected a few more passengers and lingered for the night and slipped quietly away at 7.30 a.m. next morning.

Another glimpse of Vesuvius through a mist on the port side and several beautiful islands to starboard and we were once more heading out to the high seas leaving poor shattered Italy to lick her own wounds. There was a gentle swell which surprisingly caused a lot of seasickness among the new passengers and some of the old, but British Army nurses soon pulled them from the depths of their despair. The swell persisted till the next day and strolling round by the stern rail during the afternoon I was perturbed to discover the ship's wake was non-existent. There was a gentle slapping sound as the water caressed the hull and the pulse of engine power was absent. The good ship *Dunottar Castle* had stopped.

There came a chorus of servicemen's barrack-room banter.

'She has lost her way.'

'The elastic has broken.'

'Screwdriver anyone?'

I just hoped the captain or the chief engineer were not in earshot. To the general relief the subdued throb of the engines was soon heard again, a swirl of water was churned over by the propellers and the voyage was resumed. In the quiet balmy evening the North African coast could be seen and there was a temptation to reminisce. Across there somewhere the Afrika Korps finally died. Ages ago.

Spain hove into view next day and French Morocco opposite. The Mediterranean was narrowing and also behaving perfectly. It was blissful sailing and early on February 8th the great gaunt Rock of Gibraltar lay close by. British territory at last, but the *Dunottar Castle* had no business to do there and steamed proudly into the Atlantic where she was greeted by an escort party of porpoises who accompanied us for miles, frolicking first one side and then plunging deep before reappearing the other side.

Those happy animals saw us safely on a northerly course before disappearing and there came a perceptible fall in temperature as we progressed.

Another night swinging in our hammocks and Portugal was in sight and a number of small coastal vessels bustling to and fro on their daily chores. The weather was beautiful, the sea a millpond. Even the notorious Bay of Biscay was asleep. The smooth water mirrored the sky and cloud patterns were reflected as we approached England's winter. Rain began to fall and to some this was final proof that England's shore would be seen ere long.

February 12th was the day we completed the crossing of Biscay Bay and February 12th it was when a yell rent the air and arms were pointing excitedly and there it was – a long way off yet but it could be no other but the Cornish coast. Some were talking to their friends unusually fast and loud, some seemed to doubt that what they saw was real. Others were silent as they quietly struggled with their emotions, lest they break loose in a show of unmanly tears. What a lovely ship was the *Dunottar Castle*. Bless her, she knew the way after all.

Passage up-Channel was smooth and majestic. England showed herself more and more and in sight of the Needles' lighthouse a pilot came aboard. Away over the port side – the New Forest. Opposite – the Isle of Wight and on a dull February day they looked magnificent. Passing close by Hurst Castle, anchors were dropped off the mouth of Southampton Water for the night.

We leaned on the rails to watch the ferry traffic to Cowes and the oil tankers making for the great Fawley refinery with their precious cargoes all the way from the Shatt-El Arab. They certainly reached home from there quicker than we. As our vessel swung on its anchor chain Southampton and Cowes appeared to have changed places but tomorrow was our day and doubtless all would be in its right place by then.

By dawn the *Dunottar Castle* had got herself the right way round, yanked up her anchors and glided past Calshot, Fawley and Hythe like the fine lady she was before most people on shore had finished breakfast. As she politely waited for the Southampton tugs to complete her voyage I watched the little ferries cross to Hythe and back and remembered using them in the early days of the war, and recalled walking past Bargate in the early nights of blackout and colliding with a lamppost. The ferries were named *Hotspur* then and I was glad to see that at least was unchanged.

The tugs took charge and gently pushed and chivvied us into Berth 106 between 7.00 and 8.00 a.m. Our arrival was as unheralded and unobtrusive as could be in a Union Castle liner that towered over the warehouses. There were a few dockers on the quayside who gave us a cheery wave as they looped the massive ropes over the bollards and satisfied themselves and us that the *Dunottar Castle* was safely secured to the United Kingdom.

Disembarkation was a lengthy business and we lined the rails and gave the first passengers to leave a good-natured jeer and for the ladies young and old a chorus of wolf-whistles. Post Office men came aboard and set up shop for anyone who wished to send a telegram. There were hundreds. The battalion had been told that most would be able to go home later in the day but some would have to stay a few days to effect the move into camp. Being one warned for this duty, I duly sent a telegram to my parents announcing my arrival in Southampton and added 'home in a few days'. As I awaited the great moment of setting foot on the quay my thoughts conjured up a mental picture of the telegram boy making his delivery.

Six hours elapsed before our turn came. With light hearts and happy thoughts we shouldered our kitbags and rifles and walked down the gangway and set foot on good old English concrete. In a great warehouse stood a long line of tables manned by Customs and Excise men. There was a gap in the line and, giving the Customs men looks that spoke volumes, we filed through the gap without a pause and there before us was a waiting train. With a farewell to the *Dunottar Castle* we climbed aboard and were soon speeding out into the country.

My eyes feasted on the green meadows, the hedgerows, the farms, the cows, the little stations that flowed past the windows as the train took the Royal Sussex back to Sussex. To Crowborough, in fact, where we marched in all our glory into West Camp where I was informed that I could, after all, go home that evening. Just like the Army, thought I, as I recalled the wording of the telegram, but I accepted without demur.

It was midnight when I reached home. The house was in darkness. I was not expected for a few days. Everyone was sound asleep. Front and back doors were locked.

They were roused by loud and persistent knocking.

On the front door.

The publishers hope that this book has given you enjoyable reading. Large Print Books are especially designed to be as easy to see and hold as possible. If you wish a complete list of our books please ask at your local library or write directly to:

Dales Large Print Books
Magna House, Long Preston,
Skipton, North Yorkshire.
BD23 4ND

This Large Print Book, for people
who cannot read normal print,
is published under the auspices of

THE ULVERSCROFT FOUNDATION